Beating
the Insanity
Defense

Beating the Insanity Defense

Denying the License to Kill

David M. Nissman
Brian R. Barnes
Geoffrey P. Alpert
Office of the
District Attorney,
Lane County, Oregon

LexingtonBooks
D.C. Heath and Company
Lexington, Massachusetts
Toronto

Library of Congress Cataloging in Publication Data

Nissman, David M.
  Beating the insanity defense: etc
  Bibliography: p.
  1. Criminal liability—Oregon. 2. Insanity—Jurisprudence—Oregon.
3. Defense (Criminal procedure)—Oregon. 4. Forensic psychiatry—Oregon.
I. Barnes, Brian R., joint author. II. Alpert, Geoffrey P., joint author.
III. Title. [DNLM: 1. Forensic psychiatry. 2. Expert testimony—Standards.
3. Psychological tests. 4. Malingering. 5. Homicide. W740 N726b]
KFO2966.6.N57   345.795'04   80-8028
ISBN 0-669-03943-8

Published simultaneously in Canada

Printed in the United States of America

International Standard Book Number: 0-669-03943-8

Library of Congress Catalog Card Number: 80-8028

Contents

Preface

More and more often, psychiatric defenses are being abused in the criminal-justice system. It seems inevitable, where there is little or no defense on the facts, that the defendant or his lawyer will opt for some psychiatric excuse. More liberal laws, sympathetic experts, and less-severe consequences are major reasons for this disturbing trend. This book, addressed to those who have to deal with this problem in a practical or academic manner, is designed to help prosecutors beat the mental defense and the defendant's expert witness, as well as to serve as a reference for criminal-justice educators. This endeavor is necessary since the defense very often is a hoax, enabling the guilty defendant to be set free. Once successful with the defense, the defendant may have the equivalent of a free pass to commit further crimes. To use the insanity defense effectively, the defendant must invariably have a psychiatric advocate. In order to compete successfully with the jargon of the defendant's psychiatric expert, the prosecutor needs proper weapons. This book is unique in providing the weapons and step-by-step guidance for their use to defeat the defendant's psychiatric expert in court.

By the very nature of his profession and by what he attempts to accomplish in the criminal case, the psychiatric-expert witness and his field of expertise are susceptible to impeachment. Indeed a growing number of observers of psychiatry are questioning whether psychiatric evidence should be admissible in any form in a court of law. Psychiatry, at best, is an art, not a science. The foundation upon which psychiatry is based cannot stand the test of objective, scientific scrutiny. In no other area of the law do courts allow experts to testify when their premises and conclusions are nebulous and speculative. However, unless and until the legal system recognizes and abolishes this monster it has created, the prosecution must battle with the defense expert and must rebut the aura of respectability surrounding his profession.

Beating the Insanity Defense is written as a guide to prosecutors and an introductory (although one-sided) text for students. It is basically a case study of Oregon and cites Oregon cases, but it can be generalized to any other jurisdiction.

1 The Insanity Defense: The Wild Beast of the Courtroom

Wasn't Hamlet wrong'd Laertes? Never Hamlet;
If Hamlet from himself be te'en away,
And when his not himself does wrong Laertes,
Then Hamlet does it not? Hamlet denies it.
Who does it then? His madness—

Hamlet
Act V, Scene II

Insanity is often the logic of an accurate mind overtaxed.—
Oliver Wendell Holmes,
The Autocrat at the Breakfast Table (1858)

Our legal theories premise punishment on the notion that offenders are responsible for their acts. Early philosophers who spoke of crime discussed the concept of free will and hedonistic calculations of pain versus pleasure.[1] About the middle of the eighteenth century, those who believed in this clinical theory of criminology revised their thinking to exclude the very young, the very old, and lunatics from total responsibility for their actions.[2] Clearly it was believed that some individuals were not to be held responsible, or punished, for acts that were considered crimes. The problem then, as now, is the identification of these individuals. The early courts developed a test for responsibility in the eighteenth century and called it the wild-beast test.[3] In essence, this test said that to escape punishment, the madman must be so deprived of understanding so as to know what he was doing no more than would a wild beast. As criminology and criminal law became more sophisticated and codified, more specific criteria of responsibility were identified.[4]

M'Naghten and the Insanity Defense

The courts had a difficult time determining who was and who was not criminally responsible. Many observers note that courts arbitrarily labeled defendants as insane.[5] It was not until the middle of the nineteenth century that a predominant definition of insanity was established. A British woodsman, Daniel M'Naghten, killed the male secretary to Prime Minister Robert Peel, mistaking the secretary for Peel. In his trial, M'Naghten claimed that he had a delusion that Peel's Tory party was persecuting him. M'Naghten argued that the harassment he suffered negated all power of self-control.[6] The court held that M'Naghten should be acquitted because he lacked self-control. This ruling so offended many British leaders that the House of Lords addressed a series of questions to the fifteen highest criminal-court judges in England. Fourteen of the fifteen English justices agreed that in cases where an insanity defense is raised, jurors must be told

> that everyman is presumed to be sane and to possess a sufficient degree of reason to be responsible for his crimes, until the contrary be proved to their satisfaction; and that, to establish a defense on the ground of insanity, it must be clearly proved that, at the time of the committing of the act, the party accused was labouring under such a defect of reason, from disease of the mind, as not to know the nature and quality of the act he was doing; or, if he did know it, that he did not know what he was doing was wrong.[7]

In addition, the justices added that a medical man who has heard the evidence presented in trial may be asked, as a matter of science, to comment on the testimony of witnesses and determine whether they show a mind incapable of distinguishing between right and wrong.[8] The rule of M'Naghten became commonly known as the right-or-wrong test. It established a two-part test: did the accused know right from wrong at the time of the act, and could he understand the nature of the act? This test stresses cognition, the ability to know.

In the 1980s, insanity is much more complex.[9] There have been several revisions of the definition of insanity since *M'Naghten* in numerous court cases, legislation, model codes, and many scholarly books and articles written on various aspects of insanity.[10] There have been suggestions to redefine insanity to a social definition or a medical definition.[11] There have also been suggestions to eliminate insanity as a criminal defense. Currently, however prosecuting attorneys can function properly and effectively within the constraints of the law. In this book, we first discuss insanity, then analyze its current status in criminal law, and finally describe how to beat the insanity defense.[12]

In the 1970s, the insanity defense was used in a significant number of cases in which the facts surrounding the crime were not in question. Instead in question were the defendant's mental state, the equity of holding him responsible for his acts, or the equity of subjecting him to the penalties of the criminal law.[13] We could find no empirical data on the type of defendant who pleads innocent by reason of insanity or on the type of crime that has an abnormally high rate of insanity defenses, but experience suggests that the more bizarre, eccentric crimes are often defended by claims of insanity. And public defenders and assigned counsel seem to utilize the defense of insanity more often than do retained counsel.[14] Our system of criminal justice has created a monster in the form of the insanity defense. It provides an avenue of relief for some of the most serious offenders who have been accused of committing some of the most frightening offenses.

Beyond M'Naghten: Irresistible Impulse

The case of Daniel M'Naghten was a distinct departure from the wild-beast test because it provided specific questions to be decided by the court. One of the numerous complaints about *M'Naghten* was that it institutionalized the insanity defense and made it available to any defendant with no factual defense. More specifically, *M'Naghten* focused on cognition and ignored the individual's emotions. This, it has been noted, identifies a specified and very limited definition of insanity. Through a series of case law, the irresistible-impulse test was developed and is often applied with *M'Naghten*.[15]

The irresistible-impulse test applies to a person who knew the nature, quality, and wrongfulness of his act but by reason of mental disease or defect had lost the ability to choose between right and wrong.[16] This test was formulated to examine volition or self-control. According to this theory, a person acting under an irresistible impulse is not really committing a voluntary act. Since *M'Naghten* failed to provide a defense for emotional breakdowns, about thirty of the states added the irresistible-impulse test, which states:

> The degree of insanity which will relieve the accused of the consequences of a criminal act must be such as to create in his mind an uncontrollable impulse to commit the offense charged. This impulse must be such as to override the reason and judgment and obliterate the sense of right and wrong to the extent that the accused is deprived of the power to choose between right and wrong.[17]

The impetus behind the development of the irresistible-impulse test came from the medical profession, which objected to *M'Naghten* and criticized it as forcing them to make a judgment about a legal state—insanity—rather than a behavioral state—mental illness.

Psychiatrists complained that the standards enumerated in *M'Naghten*, as well as the irresistible-impulse test, were based on faulty premises because they force the examination of special aspects of the personality, whether cognitive or volitional or both. The medical profession has argued that it is the total personality of the individual that shapes behavior and that the most appropriate question concerns what impact mental illness has had on one's total personality.[18]

By adoption of the irresistible-impulse test, the legal profession conceded several issues, but it was not yet willing to switch the determination of insanity from a legal to a behavioral perspective. Psychiatrists kept rejecting the legal tests and attempting to persuade jurists with their behavioral arguments. In 1930, Cardoza, addressing the New York Academy of Medicine, announced that he was convinced that the legal community was not handling the issue of insanity correctly and that the medical profession needed to have more influence in the determination of criminal responsibility. He agreed with the doctors that "the present legal definition of insanity has little relation to the truth of mental life."[19] His comments were loudly applauded by the medical profession but fell on deaf legal ears until the case of Monty Durham (1954).

The Durham Rule

A lower court had found Monty Durham sane when it convicted him of housebreaking. Transcripts from the trial court indicate that psychiatrists found no evidence that Durham could not tell right from wrong. On appeal, Judge David Bazelon set aside the finding because the lower court, by relying solely on the *M'Naghten* rule, had ignored psychiatric testimony that created a causal link between Durham's long history of delusions and deranged behavior and his offense. Judge Bazelon wrote that in rejecting the right-and-wrong test:

> We find that as an exclusive criterion, the right-wrong test is inadequate in that (a) it does not take sufficient account of psychic realities and scientific knowledge; and (b) it is based upon one symptom and so cannot validly be applied in all circumstances. We find that the "irresistible impulse" test is also inadequate in that it gives no recognition to mental illness characterized by brooding and reflection and so relegates acts caused by such illness to the application of the inadequate right-wrong test.[20]

This was the first time a court had overruled *M'Naghten* in favor of a behavioral definition of insanity. Judge Bazelon wrote *Durham* "to break the log jam that has been created by the old *M'Naghten* test."[21] Bazelon ordered the courts in the District of Columbia to use what was to be labeled the product rule: defendants are not guilty by reason of insanity if their criminal acts were "the product of mental disease or defect."[22] The decision was based, in part, on Bazelon's belief that psychiatrists,

> . . . if freed form M'Naghten's strait jacket, could provide extensive insights into aspects of behavior that were highly relevant to the issue of responsibility. . . . We framed our test in these words: "An accused is not criminally responsible if his unlawful act was the product of mental disease or defect."[23]

In his explanation of *Durham*, Judge Bazelon made the analogy of assessing fault in negligence cases. He admitted that the *Durham* test of sanity was not precise, just as the legal test of negligence—the failure to exercise that degree of care that would be exercised by a "reasonable man of ordinary prudence"—is not precise. He suggested that just as the jury decides the fault of negligence cases, it should decide whether the mental abnormality was either too serious or the causal connection between mental illness and behavior was too direct to impose guilt in criminal cases. The role of the medical expert was paramount in this formula. He would be able to tell the jury anything he felt was within his scope of expertise concerning the defendant's state of mind and behavior.[24]

In essence, *Durham* makes the decision on insanity primarily dependent on what psychiatrists identify as the major cause of criminality in each case. This decision was welcomed by the medical profession.[25] The product rule requires that but for causation (that is, but for the mental disease or defect), the defendant would not have committed the crime.[26] A host of criticism followed the *Durham* decision. The empirical data are not plentiful, but they reflect that pre-*Durham*, only 0.2 percent of all defendants in criminal cases in the District of Columbia were adjudged insane by its courts. After *Durham*, this statistic increased to a high of 5.1 percent in 1962, but then declined to around 2 percent after 1962.[27]

The initial increase of those found not guilty by reason of insanity in the District of Columbia could be a reflection of the heightened enthusiasm of some judges and most psychiatrists for the plea for medical interpretation of criminal behavior. Over a number of years, the persons committed to the District of Columbia's mental hospital of criminally insane had proved less amenable to treatment than had the more-psychotic patients.[28] Both as the newness of the decision subsided and the medical profession began to see that treatment was not as successful as it had hoped, the courts began to interpret *Durham* as they did *M'Naghten*: applicable only to persons with symptoms resembling those of the more typical patients in mental hospitals.[29]

During the late 1950s and early 1960s, a series of experiments designed to test the applicability of the *Durham* mandate was sponsored by the University of Chicago and Ford Foundation.[30] Thirty simulated juries were paid to listen to and rule on a tape recording of the *Durham* case testimony and argument. The jurors were randomly selected from actual jury lists, making them reasonably typical of juries in the area. After hearing the recording, ten juries were instructed according to *M'Naghten* rules, ten were given the *Durham* instructions, and the remaining ten were given a no-rule instruction, merely stating that if the defendant were insane at the time he committed the crime, he must be found not guilty by reason of insanity. The experiment was followed with a tape recording of an incest case to these thirty juries and to several additional juries. This experiment yielded the expected results. The proportion of these experimental juries finding the accused guilty by reason of insanity did not vary significantly by type of jury instructions or type of case.[31] Although what is or is not a mental disease or defect is especially important in *Durham*, this test did not seem to change the rate of conviction over a period of time. The intricate problems of causation was not easily unraveled by the medical profession.

During the heyday of the *Durham* rule, the American Law Institute (ALI) was conducting a study in criminal conduct focusing on criminal responsibility. Its report basically agreed with the irresistible-impulse test but questioned if it went far enough. The study, eventually published as part of the Model Penal Code, included the word *appreciate* rather than *know* and is neutral as to the word *criminality* or *wrongfulness*.[32] Although the final report was published in 1962, it was not widely accepted until the *Durham* rule was vacated.

As *Durham* was being encouraged in some circles, it was being criticized in others. The result of the confrontation was a series of *Durham* modifications and eventual repeal.

Modifications of the Durham Rule

Modifications to the *Durham* rule took place in the late 1950s and 1960s. For example, during a psychiatric conference at St. Elizabeth's Hospital, the attendees voted to change *sociopathy* from a nondisease to a disease.[33] Thus under *Durham*, sociopath was given a defense where none had previously existed. This change was provided by the medical commmunity raher than the legal community.[34] In *McDonald* v. *United States* (1962), the court recognized the injustice of predicating a defense on a temporary psychiatric classification, as well as the fact that the classification of a condition as a disease for psychiatric purposes is not necessarily an accurate classification for purposes of the criminal law.[35] Thus it redefined mental disease or defect in this way:

> Our purpose now is to make it very clear that neither the court nor the jury is bound by *ad hoc* definitions or conclusions as to what experts state is a disease or defect. What psychiatrists may consider a "mental disease or defect" for clinical purposes, where their concern is treatment, may or may not be the same as mental disease or defect for the jury's purpose in determining criminal responsibility.

> Consequently, for that purpose the jury should be told that a mental disease or defect includes any abnormal condition of the mind which substantially affects mental or emotional processes and substantially impairs behavior controls. The jury would consider testimony concerning the development adaptation and functioning of these processes and controls.[36]

In *Washington* v. *United States*, the court limited the role of psychiatric testimony to a description of the defendant's mental condition, leaving it to the jury to decide whether the condition was a mental disease or defect, and/or whether the crime was a product of it.[37]

Finally in *Brawner* v. *United States* (1972), the U.S. Court of Appeals repealed *Durham*.[38] In doing so, it reviewed the reasons underlying the creation of the *Durham* test eighteen years before and stated that

> a person is not responsible for criminal conduct if at the time of such conduct as a result of mental disease or defect he lacks substantial capacity either to appreciate the wrongfulness of his conduct or to conform his conduct to the requirements of the law.[39]

This *Brawner* rule differs from the ALI test because it adds:

> The term "mental disease or defect" includes any abnormal condition of the mind which substantially affects mental or emotional processes and substantially impairs behavior controls.

> In appropriate case, a defendant may request omission from instruction on defense of insanity of the phrase pertaining to lack of capacity to appreciate wrongfulness, if that particular matter is not involved on the facts, and defendant fears that jury that does not attend vigorously to the details of the instruction may erroneously suppose that the defense is lost if defendant appreciates wrongfulness.

> The introduction or proffer of past criminal and antisocial actions is not admissible as evidence of mental disease unless accompanied by expert testimony supported by showing of the concordance of a responsible segment of professional opinion, that the particular characteristics of these actions constitute convincing evidence of an underlying mental disease that substantially impairs behavioral controls.[40]

Judge Bazelon did not agree with the majority in *Brawner*, who adopted the modified ALI standard. In his opinion, concurring in part and dissenting in part, he suggested:

> The defendant is not responsible if at the time of his unlawful conduct his mental or emotional processes or behavior controls were impaired to such an extent that he cannot justly be held responsible for his act.[41]

Bazelon admits that the *Durham* experiment did not succeed in its ultimate goal of eliciting relevant psychiatric and/or psychological data for the community's determination of criminal responsibility: "The operation was a success but the patient died."[42] Bazelon went on to note that because the court's and the psychiatrist's inability to determine how the balance between morality and safety shoud be determined, the *Durham* tests must be abandoned.

The ALI Model Penal Code

The ALI test was created in its original form in 1962. Since that year it has been adopted in modified forms by most of the states. The core rule of this test of criminal responsibility states:

> (1) A person is not responsible for criminal conduct if at the time of such conduct as a result of mental disease or defect he lacks substantial capacity either to appreciate the criminality (wrongfulness) of his conduct or to conform his conduct to the requirements of law. (2) As used in this article, the terms "mental disease or defect" do not include an abnormality manifested only by repeated criminal or otherwise antisocial conduct.[43]

This test is a fusion of the *M'Naghten* and *Durham* rules. It modifies *M'Naghten* to such a great extent that the potency of *M'Naghten* is utterly depleted, while the clarity with which it could be applied is eliminated. The new test was written so as to relieve the shortcomings and inflexibility of *M'Naghten* by a subtle shift in linguistics. (ALI substituted the word *appreciate* for *know* and is neutral as to the words *criminality* or *wrongfulness*.) The intention of this word change was to incorporate the concept of emotional awareness as well as the intellectual awareness to be considered in assessing the mental state of the accused. The ALI test requires only a substantial incapacity, thereby extending to the defendant a less stringent test of mental illness. It also removed the moral concept of determining right from wrong from the medical profession while rigidly maintaining a legal concept of insanity.

The second section of the ALI test is designed to bar the sociopath from raising the defense. The ALI commentary to the code explains this provision:

> Paragraph (2) of section 4.01 is designed to exclude from the concept of "mental disease or defect" the case of so-called "psychopathic personality." The reason for the exclusion is that, as the Royal Commission put it, psychopathy "is a statistical abnormality; that is to say, the psychopath differs from a normal person only quantitatively or in degree, not qualitatively; and the diagnosis of psychopathic personality does not carry with it any explanation of the cause of the abnormality." While it may not be feasible to formulate a definition of "disease," there is much to be said for excluding a condition that is manifested only by the behavior phenomena that must, by hypothesis, be the result of disease for irresponsibility to be established. Although British psychiatrists have agreed, on the whole, that psychopathy should not be called "disease," there is considerable difference of opinion on the point in the United States. Yet it does not seem useful to contemplate the litigation of what is essentially a matter of terminology; nor is it right to have the legal result rest upon the resolution of a dispute of this kind.[44]

Currently twenty-two states still follow the *M'Naghten* rule;[45] eleven state jurisdictions use the irresistible-impulse test;[46] two states employ the *Durham* rule;[47] and fifteen states have adopted a version of the ALI Model Penal Code test.[48] Although there have been several alterations of the ALI Model Penal Code that have been adopted by various federal circuits, most jurisdictions adhere fairly closely to the original ALI test.[49]

Abolition of the Insanity Defense

At least two major arguments suggest the abolition of the insanity plea.[50] The first includes allegations that the insanity defense is used to allow the incarceration of innocent but dangerous persons. This would include individuals who have committed dangerous acts but who lack sufficient mental capacity to be held responsible.[51] This argument suggests that this is an illegitimate purpose and should be removed. Instead a defendant should argue that he lacked mens rea rather than that he is not guilty by reason of insanity.[52]

The second argument, which is more complex, is that the insanity defense seeks to draw a line that is impossible to establish. The advocates of this argument hold that the concept of mental disease is virtually impossible to determine. They suggest that the real question is how mentally unbalanced a person must be in order to have a defense. This position represents a certain unfairness in that it gives a complete defense to a person based on one side of the line and no defense at all to a person who is just on the other side.[53] And determining who is on which side of the line is difficult, if not impossible. Commenting on psychiatric testimony, lawyer and sociologist Abraham Blumberg has noted:

> At the very least, in a trial situation, its adversary features would also include psychiatric testimony favorable to the accused's position. The psychiatric profession of course chafes under the situation. The spectacle of two or more qualified (and even at times eminent) psychiatrists making diametrically opposed statements in a courtroom about an accused's prior and present mental condition has been viewed with dismay by members of the profession. It has also helped to present psychiatry to the world as something other than a "science," despite its own science-building model and its claims of scientific impartiality.[54]

Blumberg also charges that "psychiatric testimony is for sale" and that some psychiatrists earn a major portion of their incomes from testifying in the courtroom.[55] Blumberg is not necessarily accusing psychiatrists of being corrupt; he is simply pointing to the "incredible flexibility and vacuousness of its diagnostic labels and pigeonholes."[56]

The freedom and ungoverned state of the psychiatric profession has been criticized for years, but it was not until Professor Rosenhan of Stanford University experimented with psychiatric diagnoses that reliable empirical data were made available.[57] Rosenhan set up an experiment in which eight sane people deliberately got themselves admitted at various times to a dozen different mental hospitals. The pseudopatients were instructed to report that they had heard voices, but once hospitalized they behaved in a normal fashion, reporting no further symptoms. They did have frank and open discussions with the medical staff and did mention their likes, dislikes, concerns, and disappointments. In fact, several of the pseudopatients told the staff that at times they disliked their children and spouses. Apparently these comments and other observations convinced the medical staffs that the pseudopatients were schizophrenic. Rosenhan reports that other mental patients accused his pseudopatients of being spies for the hospital staff. It appeared that the committed patients were able to identify the fake patients better than the staff could.

Rosenhan's patients received a wide variety of medications and were hospitalized between seven and fifty-two days (nineteen days on average). Each was released with the diagnosis of schizophrenia in remission. After publicity of the initial study, many in the psychiatric profession claimed that Rosenhan was less than professional in his research endeavor. Rosenhan responded by saying he would send an unspecified number of pseudopatients to one of the best mental hospitals in the country over a three-month period and asked the staff to rate the probability of each new entrant's being a pseudopatient. The hospital admitted 193 new patients during the three months. For 41 of the patients, at least one staff member expressed "high confidence" that the new admittee was a pseudopatient. Licensed psychiatrists expressed "high confidence" for 23 of the new patients. When asked how many pseudopatients were sent to the hospital, Rosenhan answered, *"None!"*

Although this study may have methodological problems, it certainly demonstrates that psychiatry is more of an art than a science.[58] The data certainly contribute to the position that the insanity plea is often misused and that decisions of not guilty by reason of insanity are often miscarriages of justice.

Notes

1. Raffaele Garofalo, *Criminology*, trans. Robert W. Miller (Boston: Little, Brown, 1914).

2. Don Gibbons, *Society, Crime and Criminal Careers* (Englewood Cliffs, N.J.: Prentice-Hall, 1977).

3. *Ferrers Case*, 19 Howard State Trials 886 (1760).

4. J. Hall, "Psychiatry and Criminal Responsibility," *Yale Law Journal* 65 (May 1956):761-785.

5. Abraham Blumberg, *Criminal Justice* (Chicago: Quandrangle Books, 1970)

6. *M'Naghten's Case*, 8 Eng. Rep. 718 (H.L. 1843).

7. Ibid., p. 722.

8. Ibid., and Nigel Walker, *Crime and Sanity in England: The Historical Perspective* (Edinburgh, Scotland: University Press, 1968).

9. For a thorough analysis of insanity, mental disease, and related concepts, see *The International Encyclopedia of the Social Sciences* (New York: Macmillan, 1968), 10:127-214.

10. See Appendix F, "Bibliography of Insanity Literature."

11. G. Morris, *Insanity Defense—A Blueprint for Legislative Reform* (Lexington, Mass.: D.C. Heath and Company, 1975), and R. Slovenko, "Developing Law on Competency to Stand Trial," *Journal of Psychiatry and Law* 5 (Summer 1977):165-200.

12. *Psychiatry and the Criminal Courts* (Los Angeles: District Attorney's Office, n.d.).

13. Arnold Lowey, *Criminal Law* (St. Paul: West Publishing Co., 1975).

14. We were not able to locate any jurisdictions that compile completely accurate statistical data in such a fashion. Conventional wisdom, informal interviews, and practical experience lead us to believe that the insanity defense is most often used in somewhat unique crimes. Also it takes much less time to use an insanity defense than to challenge factual allegations. See M. Colvin and G. Sweeney, *Representing the Mentally Retarded—A Defense Lawyer's Manual* (Baltimore: Maryland State Bar Association, 1978); Daniel Glaser, *Crime in Our Changing Society* (New York: Holt, Rinehart and Winston, 1978); J. Gleick, "Getting Away with Murder," *New Times*, 21 August, 1978, pp. 21-27; G.P. Lynch, "Insanity Defense," *Chicago Bar Record* 55 (March-April 1974):210-214, 216-217; H. Steadman, *Beating a Rap?—Defendants Found Incompetent to Stand Trial* (Chicago: University of Chicago Press, 1979), and J. Whatley, "Indigents and the Insanity Defense," *Law and Psychology Review* 3 (Fall 1977):115-134.

15. Hazel Kerper, *Introduction to the Criminal Justice System* (St. Paul: West Publishing Co., 1979).

16. *Parson* v. *State*, 81 Ala. 577, 2 So. 854 (1887).

17. *Smith* v. *United States*, 36 F.2d 548, 549 (1929). There is, however, some dispute as to how irresistible the impulse must be. An extreme definition suggests that the defense is not available unless the defendant would have committed the crime even if there had been a "policeman at [his] elbow."

U.S. v. *Kunak*, 5 U.S.C.M.A. 346 (1954). Other courts merely ask whether the defendant had the capacity to control his conduct. *S.* v. *White*, 270 F.2d (N.M. 1954). In sum, irresistible impulse is not one test, but many tests. At its strictest, it does not differ significantly from *M'Naghten*; at its most liberal interpretation, it approximates *Durham*.

18. Kerper, *Introduction*; Lowey, *Criminal Law*; Hall, "Psychiatry and Criminal Responsibility"; "Insanity and the Criminal Law," *University of Chicago Law Review* 22 (Winter 1955): 317-404; and Abraham Goldstein, *The Insanity Defense* (New Haven: Yale University Press, 1967).

19. Benjamin Cardoza, *Law and Literature and Other Essays and Addresses* (New York: Harcourt and Brace, 1931).

20. *Durham* v. *United States*, 214 F.2d 862, 874 (D.C. Cir. 1954).

21. David Bazelon, "The Morality of the Criminal Law," *Southern California Law Review* 49 (March 1976):385-405; see David Bazelon, "Psychiatrists and the Advisory Process," *Scientific American* 230 (June 1974):18-23.

22. *Durham* v. *United States*; see *Carter* v. *United States*, 252 F.2d 608 (D.C. Cir. 1957).

23. Bazelon, "Morality," p. 390.

24. Ibid.

25. Lewis Danziger, "A Psychiatrist's View of Insanity as a Defense in Criminal Cases," *Marquette Law Review* 40 (Spring 1977):406-412; Hall, "Psychiatry and Criminal Responsibility"; Ben Karpman, "On Reducing Tensions and Bridging the Gaps between Psychiatry and the Law," *Journal of Criminal Law, Criminology and Police Science* 48 (July-August 1958):164-174; "Insanity and the Criminal Law".

26. This "but for" causation has been criticized as too complex and requiring mental gymnastics that cannot be accomplished. "How can one say what one would have done had his mental condition not been what it was? We just don't know." Lowey, *Criminal Law*, p. 223.

27. The 2 percent figure approximates other jurisdictions' statistics that operate with *M'Naghten* or *M'Naghten* and the irresistible-impulse test. The inflated figure can be attributed to the halo effect often found in highly publicized situations. In this situation, extensive professional debate on *Durham* took place among lawyers and psychiatrists. See Lowey, *Criminal Law*.

28. Samuel Yochelson and Stanton Samenow, *The Criminal Personality* (New York: Jason Aronson, 1975), vol. 1.

29. Richard Arens, "The Durham Rule in Action," *Law and Society Review* 1 (June 1967):41-80; C. Ray Jeffery, *Criminal Responsibility and Mental Disease* (Springfield, Ill.: Charles C. Thomas, 1967); and R. Arens and H. Laswell, *Make Mad the Guilty* (Springfield, Ill.: Charles C. Thomas, 1969).

30. Rita Simon, *The Jury and the Defense of Insanity* (Boston: Little, Brown, 1967).

31. Ibid. There was, however, significantly more discussion among jurors with the *Durham* instructions. There jurors did end in hung juries more often than other juries did.

32. See John MacDonald, *Psychiatry and the Law* (Springfield, Ill.: Charles C. Thomas, 1976).

33. Yochelson and Samenow, *Criminal Personality*, vol. 1. See also *Overholser* v. *Lynch*, 109 U.S. App. D.C. 404 (1959), which took a big step toward therapeutic protectionism and authoritarianism by asserting the responsibility and duty of society to require an offender to undergo therapy rather than punishment. Although Lynch could have been sentenced only to twelve months and probably would have been placed on probation, he was committed to a mental institution for an indeterminant period, where he committed suicide. See *Overholser* v. *Lynch*, 369 U.S. 705 (1962), and Richard Arens, "Due Process and the Rights of the Mentally Ill: The Strange Case of Frederick Lynch," *Catholic University Law Review* 13 (October 1964): 246-259.

34. *Blocker* v. *United States*, 274 F.2d 572 (D.C. Cir. 1959).

35. *McDonald* v. *United States*, 312 F.2d 847 (D.C. Cir. 1962).

36. Ibid., p. 851.

37. *Washington* v. *United States*, 390 F.2d 444 (D.C. Cir. 1967).

38. *Brawner* v. *United States*, 471 F.2d 969 (D.C. Cir. 1972).

39. Ibid.

40. Ibid.

41. Ibid., p. 1032.

42. Bazelon, "Morality," p. 395.

43. Quoted in MacDonald, *Psychiatry and the Law*, p. 72.

44. ALI Model Penal Code, subsection 4.01 Commentary, Tentative Draft No. 4 (1955), p. 160.

45. Arizona, Arkansas, Delaware, Florida, Hawaii, Iowa, Kansas, Louisiana, Mississippi, Nebraska, Nevada, New Jersey, New York (uses *appreciate* rather than *know*), North Carolina, North Dakota, Oklahoma, Pennsylvania, Rhode Island, South Carolina, South Dakota, Tennessee, and Washington.

46. Alabama, Colorado, Georgia, Michigan, Minnesota, Missouri, New Mexico, Ohio, Texas, Virginia, and Wyoming.

47. Maine and New Hampshire.

48. California, Connecticut, Idaho, Illinois, Indiana, Maryland, Massachusetts, Oregon, Utah, Vermont, West Virginia, and Wisconsin. Alaska, Montana, and Kentucky have adopted modified versions of the Model Penal Code test.

49. *United States* v. *Charles Freeman*, 357 F.2d 606 (2d Cir. 1966), and *U.S.* v. *Currens*, 290 F.2d 751 (3d Cir. 1961); see MacDonald, *Psychiatry and the Law*. One of the major revisions includes the concept of diminished responsibility. Under this rule, the offense can be reclassified to permit a

lesser penalty if the mental capacity of the offender is thought to have been partially impaired at the time of the crime. See "Criminal Law—Re-examination of Tests for Criminal Responsibility," *Michigan Law Review* 57 (May 1955):463-972.

50. Lowey, *Criminal Law.*

51. This can be accompanied by civilly committing a person who is found not guilty by reason of insanity. Although most jurisdictions can return a verdict of guilty, not guilty, or not guilty by reason of insanity, a few jurisdictions (most notably California) bifurcate the trial by having the jury determine whether the defendant is guilty; then another jury determines whether the defendant was insane at the time the crime was committed.

52. Nancy Juren, "The Insanity Defense in Criminal Trials," *Suffolk University Law Review* 10 (Summer 1967):1037-1063, and Nicholas Kittrie, *The Right to Be Different* (Baltimore: Penguin Press, 1974).

53. That is, in the absence of some type of partial insanity (such as premeditation) that might negate a specific element of the crime.

54. Blumberg, *Criminal Justice*, p. 148.

55. Ibid., p. 149.

56. Ibid., and H. Morrison, *Role, Function and Expectations of the Psychiatric Expert Witness* (New York: Practicing Law Institute, 1978).

57. D.L. Rosenhan, "On Being Sane in Insane Places," *Science* 197 (January 1973):250-258.

58. Geoffrey P. Alpert, review of Yochelson and Samenow, *The Criminal Personality. The Criminal Justice Review* 2 (Fall 1977):137-139, and Lee Karpman, "On Reducing Tensions and Bridging the Gaps between Psychiatry and the Law," *Journal of Criminal Law, Criminology and Police Science* 48 (July-August 1958):164-174.

2 Preparing the State's Case

The best approach for a prosecutor in a criminal trial is to preclude the defense from raising the issue of insanity. The most effective method of doing this is by conducting a thorough investigation of all potential witnesses who may appear during the trial.

When the defendant is arrested, the prosecutor should advise all officers who have or will have contact with him to record their observations, no matter how trivial they may seem. They should do this in all mental cases regardless of whether the defendant confesses. For example, even if the defendant invokes his rights, this fact may be important and admissible to show that the defendant acted rationally near the time of the crime. If possible, the defendant's actions should be videotaped when arrested. Many mental defenses can be defeated at the outset by timely videotape showing him acting and speaking normally shortly after he has committed the crime. It is useful to have testimony regarding these aspects:

1. Defendant's physical condition, particularly whether he is intoxicated.
2. Defendant's ability to follow the directions of the officer (such as "raise your hands" or "drop the gun").
3. Defendant's orientation as to time, place, and his status.
4. Defendant's reactions, responses, and questions as to whether they are appropriate to his situation.
5. Defendant's ability to carry out basic functions, such as eating, drinking, and using the toilet.
6. Defendant's habits in custody regarding personal hygeine, reading books, playing cards or other games, associations with other prisoners, and guards. Observers should be on the lookout for any complaints by the defendant about his status or jail conditions or his selectivity in what he eats or does while in custody.

These are just a sampling of the kinds of information that can help show the defendant's responsibility for his actions. The range is limited only by one's imagination.

In most cases, the state is interested primarily in the defendant's confession to the crime, but this is not necessarily so in a mental case. In fact, if the defendant can be caught lying about his involvement or about anything else, this may be the most valuable evidence in the long run. A jury will be reluctant to acquit when the prosecution can cast doubt on the defendant's credibility, since his psychiatrist will almost always be relying on the premise that the defendant is relating a truthful history. In addition, the more the defendant lies to minimize his guilt, the more likely the jury will believe that he had the capacity to appreciate the wrongfulness of his actions.

Shortly after the defendant's arrest, investigators should contact his family, friends, and acquaintances concerning his mental state. The first reaction of family members usually is that the defendant is a good person, has caused little trouble, and has never had any mental or emotional problems (although in cases in which the defendant has had a long history of mental problems, the response may be different). In the majority of cases in which the defense is a hoax created by psychiatrists and crafty defense attorneys, this kind of pursuit provides invaluable lay evidence of sanity. And if some of those witnesses later testify for the defendant, the prosecutor at least will be able to impeach them by their prior inconsistent statements.

The prosecutor should keep a record of all visits to the defendant in jail and should contact jail personnel regarding their conversations with him. One good example is a Lane County, Oregon, case in which a defendant accused of armed robbery raised the defense of insanity. The deputy district attorney put the court transport deputy on the witness stand and asked about any conversations with the defendant. These conversations tended to show that the defendant knew what was going on around him. For example, when the deputy was discussing the defendant's thoughts about the chances of his defense succeeding, the defendant responded, "My lawyer knows what he's doing. He can get me off. I'll just let him do his job."[1]

Harlan M. Goulett has recounted an instance in which this kind of testimony proved invaluable:[2]

A police officer was able to recall and describe vividly each movement, gesture, and utterance of the suspect at the time of his arrest. The reactions were, at least in the mind of a jury, very normal. The suspect had been arrested in the kitchen of his home. He later asked permission of the officer guarding him to go with his mother into the living room to talk with her. Ordinarily unimportant, this kind of behavior in an insanity case shows excellent contact with reality and a comprehension of his situation. The officer stayed within hearing distance of the living room conversation. The suspect indicated he wanted privacy, then raised his shackled hands and told the officer, "Don't worry, I ain't goin' no place." Again, comprehension and contact with reality. Apparently the suspect was sane enough to understand the officer was unwilling to risk an escape attempt.

In the same case a former wife of the defendant visited him in jail. Her visit occurred within hours of the examination by a defense psychiatrist. This psychiatrist testified the defendant was insane at the time of the examination and at the time of the crime. But this opinion was weakened considerably by the testimony of the ex-wife. She also testified that he appeared withdrawn, unable to understand, and claimed he did not know why he was in jail. However, as she got up to leave the jail, she told him that it was a good story and he should stick with it. By way of response, he raised his eyes from the floor, a grin spread over his face and he gave her a broad wink.[3]

In another Lane County case, the defendant was in jail for extorting $18,000 from a bank manager by kidnapping and holding his wife as a hostage. The defendant had no defense on the facts and faced eighty-five years in jail for the multiple crimes committed, so his attorney decided to use an insanity defense. The defense attorney sought out a local psychiatrist known for his ability to present an opinion excluding responsibility. Despite a past mental history and some fairly convincing bizarre behavior prior to trial, the defendant pleaded guilty to all charges. The defense had been informed that a jailer had overheard the defendant stating to another prisoner, "I'll get them on a crazy trial. I can act real crazy if I want to."[4]

In addition to personal contacts, the investigation should produce all medical, school, employment, armed-service, and criminal-history records of the defendant. The more evidence gathered to build a foundation of sanity, the harder the defense will have to work to damage the state's case.

This investigation should take particular note of any behavior of the defendant that appears goal oriented at or near the time of the crime. This conduct, when established during the state's case in chief, will help dispel the notion that defendant is crazy before the defense calls a witness. This evidence also tends to have more credibility since psychiatric evaluations are conducted after the crime and must therefore be, at best, an educated guess concerning defendant's abilities to act rationally during the crime.

It must be remembered that the defendant is presumed sane. The jury, once convinced that the defendant has committed a crime, will be reluctant to exonerate him. There has been an ongoing debate as to the worth of psychiatric testimony in terms of credibility with the jury. The results may differ from state to state and county to county depending on the education and financial background of the community.

Lay witnesses can be at least as effective as psychiatric witnesses, especially if the former have had long associations with the defendant. In an Oregon case, the defendant was convicted in a nonjury trial of third-degree rape.[5] At the trial the defendant put forward psychiatric testimony. In rebuttal, the state did not produce psychiatric testimony but instead called five lay witnesses who were intimately acquainted with the defendant to rebut evidence that the defendant was insane. On appeal the defendant challenged the admissibility of lay testimony on the issue of sanity. The Oregon Court of Appeals affirmed the conviction:

The sole defense was insanity. During defendant's case, one expert medical witness testified that defendant was insane, i.e., that defendant lacked "substantial capacity . . . to conform his conduct to the requirements of law" within the meaning of ORS 161.295. In rebuttal, the state called five witnesses who had been co-workers with and friends of defendant for periods of two to six years. Over objection, all of them testified that, based on their experiences with and observations of defendant, he did not lack substantial capacity to conform his conduct to the requirements of law. The trial court found the sum of . . . [the] lay testimony . . . to be more convincing that that of the psychiatrist.[6]

In a well-known insanity case in Colorado, the defendant pleaded not guilty by reason of insanity to the charge of kidnapping.[7] At the trial the state put forth no psychiatric evidence but did use one lay witness to comment on the defendant's sanity. The defense introduced psychiatric testimony, but the defendant was found guilty by the jury. On appeal he charged that the trial court should have directed the jury to find him not guilty by reason of insanity due to the "unrefuted" psychiatric evidence in his behalf.

> The contention that at the conclusion of the sanity trial the trial court committed error when it refused to direct the jury to return a verdict of insanity is without merit. There is, at the outset, *a presumption of sanity*. The People then introduced the testimony of the lay witness, Durham, to the effect that Rupert was sane. It is quite true that thereafter, by way of defense, a psychiatrist did testify that in his opinion Rupert was insane as of the date of the alleged commission of the crime. But all this did was pose a disputed issue of fact to be resolved by the trier of the facts. The instant factual situation is somewhat akin to that found in *Arridy* v. *People*, 103 Colo. 29, 82 P.2d 757. In that case we held that there was sufficient evidence to support a jury's determination that Arridy was sane, even though the medical testimony was to the contrary. And in the *Arridy* case, as in the instant one, the supporting evidence came from lay witnesses, as opposed to expert testimony.[8]

It is very likely that lay witnesses will be more persuasive than paid experts with lay jurors. Since a presumption of sanity exists, a strong foundation of criminal awareness should be built upon the testimony of lay witnesses.

Notes

1. *State* v. *Ernest Banuelos*, Lane County Circuit Court No. 76-274.
2. Harlan Goulett, *The Insanity Defense in Criminal Trials* (St. Paul: West, 1975), p. 72.
3. *State of Minnesota* v. *David Ohaemers*, Hennepin County, Criminal File No. 47459, cited by ibid.

4. *State* v. *Ronald Lemco*, Lane County Circuit Court No. 77-4402.
5. *State* v. *Van Dolah*, 14 Or. App. 125, 512, P.2d 1013 (1973).
6. Ibid., p. 126.
7. *Rupert* v. *People*, 429 P.2d 276 (1967).
8. Ibid., p. 277.

3 Developing a Strategy

As soon as it appears likely that insanity will be raised as an issue at trial, the prosecutor should start developing a strategy to counter the defense. Three important areas should be considered in order to arrive at the best tactical choice: the facts of the particular case, the mental-responsibility laws of the jurisdiction, and whether the case will be tried to a court or to a jury.

Facts of the Case

The facts of the case are the most important aspect in the prosecutor's consideration of a potential strategy because they will be the most persuasive information that the jury will weigh when deciding the issue of sanity. There are several reasons why this is true. To begin with, the court will instruct the jurors that they are to determine what the defendant's mental state was at the time of the crime. The only direct evidence that they will have on that issue will be the facts of the crime. Psychiatric interviews are conducted after the crime and thus cannot be as useful to the jury as the facts themselves. Furthermore, even without the court's instruction, the facts will paint a picture of the defendant's mind. If a defendant kills a clerk during a robbery, the motive—to get the money—is comprehensible. Where a rational, albeit criminal, motive can be established, it will be difficult for the defendant to convince the jury to exonerate him.

It is even more difficult for a defendant to prove insanity in a felony-murder situation such as this. Felony murder is a natural consequence of a robbery and one that a jury can understand readily. The defense may try to show that the motive for the robbery was based on defective reasoning, but then the prosecution can use the murder to show that the defendant realized the criminality of his act of robbery and conformed his behavior to effectuate his escape. On the other hand, if the fact pattern itself tends to show the presence of a defective or diseased mind, it may warrant a different kind of strategy.[1]

The Law of the Jurisdiction

The mental-responsibility laws of the jurisdiction are also important in helping to determine an effective strategy in combating the insanity defense.

Psychiatric Examinations

Before deciding whether to employ a psychiatrist for the state, a primary question concerns how useful the psychiatrist will be. What can the doctor accomplish, and what information can he lawfully obtain from the defendant?

In Oregon, the state was granted the right to conduct a psychiatric examination of a defendant who raised the insanity defense in *State* v. *Phillips*.[2] This rule was codified by the Oregon legislature in 1971:

> Upon filing of notice or the introduction of evidence by the defendant as provided in subsection (3) of ORS 161.309, the State shall have the right to have at least one psychiatrist of its selection examine the defendant. The State shall file notice with the court of its intention to have the defendant examined. Upon filing of the notice, the court, in its discretion, may order the defendant committed to a state institution or any other suitable facility for observation and examination as it may designate for a period not to exceed 30 days. If the defendant objects to the psychiatrist chosen by the State, the court for good cause shown may direct the State to select a different psychiatrist.

This rule was immediately modified by *Shepard* v. *Bowe*.[3] In *Shepard* the state moved to have the defendant examined by a psychiatrist, and the trial judge ordered the defendant to answer all questions put to him by the state's psychiatrist, including some concerning the defendant's conduct at or near the time of the crime. The trial judge also ruled that the defendant could not have his attorney present during the psychiatric interview. The Oregon Supreme Court ruled that this procedure violated the defendant's Fifth Amendment privilege against self-incrimination. The court ordered that the state could not force a defendant to answer questions posed by the state's psychiatrist concerning the defendant's conduct at or near the time of the alleged crime. By implication, the defendant also has the right to have his attorney present during the examination. However, the court did not rule specifically on this point, and having counsel present is more of a custom than a judicially promulgated rule of law.

When the Oregon court announced *Shepard*, it went against the weight of authority in the United States. The rule followed most frequently was announced by the New Jersey Supreme Court in *State* v. *Whitlow*:

> To allow the accused to obtain his own expert, and, after a private and unlimited conference with him and examination by him, to plead insanity, and then put forward the privilege against self-incrimination to frustrate like activities by the prosecution, is to balance the competing interests unfairly and disproportionately against the public.[4]

State v. *Whitlow* stands for the principle that the state should be allowed to give a defendant a complete psychiatric examination when the defendant raises the issue of insanity. This examination includes questions concerning the defendant's conduct at or near the time of the alleged crime. *Whitlow* is followed frequently and cited in almost all jurisdictions, while *Shepard* v. *Bowe* does not seem to have attracted much of a following.[5]

Another tactical question concerning the psychiatric examination is what effect the defendant's refusal to submit to a psychiatric examination will have on his defense. In *State ex rel. Johnson* v. *Richardson*, the Oregon Supreme Court held that if a defendant refuses to answer questions put to him by the state's psychiatrist, the defense of insanity will be stricken.[6]

Admissibility of Psychiatric Evidence

Psychiatric evidence is admissible at various stages of the trial in different jurisdictions. In those that allow a complete psychiatric examination by the state, the evidence is admissible only in rebuttal.[7] In connection with the use of psychiatric evidence a companion issue arises: the timely disclosure of psychiatric reports. By statute, many jurisdictions require pretrial disclosure of reports of witnesses, including experts, that a party intends to call at trial. Thus for effective results, the prosecution should file a pretrial motion requesting discovery of defense psychiatric reports and the data upon which the final report is based.

The case of *State* v. *Roger Dyke* illustrates the use of data in destroying the credibility of psychiatry, as well as getting the whole truth from the expert.[8] Dyke was committed to the state hospital for the criminally insane after shooting his mother. Within a year the hospital believed he was no longer dangerous and requested his release. The official hospital report supported this belief and indicated that Dyke had had no problems. The presecution obtained the treatment notes of the hospital, however, and discovered that just weeks prior to the court hearing, Dyke had been out on a day pass and had attempted to buy a gun at a local sporting-goods store. When confronted with the information by the prosecutor, the hospital psychiatrist acknowledged that Dyke had a few problems. In fact, Dyke had admitted he wanted the gun to shoot both his treating psychiatrist and his social counselor at the hospital.

The Burden of Proof

Another element worth considering in picking a strategy is who bears the burden of proof. In the federal courts, the government has the burden of proof, and the standard is beyond a reasonable doubt.[9] Many state courts, however, give the defendant the burden of proof, a product of the common law first enunciated in *M'Naghten*. The procedure of making the defendant bear this burden with respect to insanity was constitutionally sanctioned by the U.S. Supreme Court in *Leland* v. *Oregon*.[10] In *Leland* the court found that the existence or nonexistence of legal insanity bears no necessary relationship to the existence or nonexistence of the required mental elements of the crime.

Although it is constitutionally permissible to place the burden of proving insanity on the defendant, it is unconstitutional to place the burden of proving extreme emotional disturbance or heat of passion on the defendant. This rule was announced by the Supreme Court in *Mullaney* v. *Wilbur* on the grounds that an element of murder is that it was not committed in the heat of passion and that the state must prove every element of the crime beyond a reasonable doubt.[11]

It is important to separate the issues before deciding on a strategy. If the issue is insanity, the defense bears the burden. If the issue is extreme emotional disturbance, the state must be prepared to disprove extreme emotional disturbance beyond a reasonable doubt.[12]

The Bifurcated Trial

In several jurisdictions, cases in which insanity is raised are handled in two separate trials. The first is the guilt phase, in which the issue is whether the defendant committed the act. If the defendant is found guilty, a second phase, the penalty phase, becomes necessary to determine whether the defendant was legally insane at the time of the crime.[13] In these jurisdictions, the prosecutor may want to use all available psychiatric evidence because insanity is the only issue in the penalty phase of the trial.

Court or Jury?

A fundamental question in an insanity trial concerns who will be the trier of fact. If the case is tried to a court, psychiatric evidence should probably be used, since judges are generally more impressed with psychiatric testimony than are juries. This view is substantiated by a report compiled by the Office of the U.S. Attorney. The report reveals that in the district court for the District of Columbia from 1964 to 1970, 19 verdicts of not guilty by reason of insanity were returned by juries, while 262 verdicts of not guilty by reason of insanity were returned in cases tried to a court.[14]

If the case is to be tried to a jury, it is important for the prosecution to diagnose the composition of the jury. Juries in some counties may have a propensity for finding defendants not guilty by reason of insanity because of a widespread respect for psychiatrists in that community. In this event, the state should use psychiatric testimony. (In such communities, it might be useful for the state to mount a public-relations campaign to dispel the myths about psychiatric testimony.)

The Strategy

In light of considerations concerning the facts, the law, and the trier of fact, the prosecution must pick a strategy that will tactically counter the defense of insanity. A variety of approaches are possible.

The Bullet Method

The simplest approach to an insanity defense is to meet the defense without using a psychiatrist. The key for the prosecution is to build a factual scenario depicting the defendant as a clear-thinking individual before any evidence of insanity is introduced. Lay witnesses who know the defendant can be used to support the contention of sanity. When the defense puts a psychiatrist on the stand, the prosecution should subject the witness to vigorous cross-examination. Cross-examination may be aided by testing the defendant psychologically after the defense psychiatrist's report is available. The results from such tests often will contradict what is in the defense psychiatric report. (The tests may also contradict each other.) Effective use of the tests will help impeach the defense psychiatrist. In the rare instance where all of the tests and the psychiatrist agree, it is useful to get the psychiatrist to agree with the results and even to rely on them. Then the prosecution can attack the tests, and by analogy the psychiatrist's opinion will lose its credibility.

In argument, the prosecution should stress the fact that the lay witnesses knew the defendant at or near the time of the crime, while the psychiatrist met and interviewed the defendant only much later. If the state has done an effective job of impeaching the expert, the lay witnesses should be more credible than the expert to the jury.

This is the most adventurous and dangerous strategy to use. For those who mastered the art of psychology, the risk involved should decrease. However, the only expert psychiatric evidence in front of the jury will come from the defendant. This fact may end up leaving the state out in the cold. This strategy has cost in its favor because it is very inexpensive.

The Double Cross

An offshoot of the bullet method is the double cross. In a case in which the defense psychiatric report divulges incriminating statements made by the defendant, the defense psychiatrist in the case in chief should be called to help prove the crime. There may be a hearsay objection, but this is easily met and overcome by citing the common-law rule admitting admissions by a party opponent.[15] In addition, the defense attorney may argue that a defendant-psychiatrist communication is a confidential communication. However, most states protect only the communication between a regular physician and his patient.[16] The statutes often protect communication between a licensed psychologist and his patient but often fail to specify psychiatrists. In any case, a privilege is waived when the privileged matter is disclosed to third parties. Therefore the privilege objection may be overcome, and the evidence can be used to cement a case in chief.

In a related situation, a psychiatrist employed by the defense may write a report showing that the defendant has some mental or emotional problems that do not give rise to a mental defense under the law. Or the defense psychiatrist may give the defendant a colorable defense, which is based on incorrect facts. In these situations, it may be advisable to discuss the evaluation with the psychiatrist. He might change his opinion and the prosecutor can put him on the stand. There is nothing more devastating to an insanity defense than having the only psychiatrist testify that the defendant does not have a mental defense. However, it is always dangerous for the prosecution to point out to the adverse expert the weakness of his conclusion prior to trial, for the prosecutor may be the one who ends up being the victim of the double cross at trial.

The prosecution may also determine that the defense attorney has sent the defendant to a psychiatrist who will not be a witness at trial. Generally this means that the psychiatrist has found the defendant sane. If such a psychiatrist can be utilized as a prosecution witness, the defense will collapse.

One-on-One

The most widely used method in insanity trials is the one-on-one method in which each side has a psychiatrist relating a conflicting opinion of the defendant's mental state. This method is sometimes referred to as a battle of the experts. In this instance it is important for the prosecution to work closely with its psychiatrist, supplying him with all police reports, coroner's reports, and background information that can be gathered. This psychiatrist should be apprised of every factual aspect of the case and should spend as much time with the defendant as possible in order to avoid his being impeached by the fact that he reached his opinion after seeing the defendant one time briefly. Nothing can destroy his credibility quicker. Jurors are justified in concluding that in such important matters more is required.

These procedures are important in order to build the most solid foundation possible for the psychiatrist's opinion, which will protect him from possible impeachment. The prosecution's knowledge will also enhance its possibilities of impeaching the opposing expert. It should always try to lead the opposing psychiatrist over to its own viewpoint. If its case is good and the opposing expert obstinately and repeatedly refuses to agree, he may lose his credibility with the jury. Lay witnesses are also useful here to lend support to the state's psychiatrist.

The Ambush

This method is the newest and most innovative approach to insanity defenses and the one that requires the most time and education. The purpose of the ambush approach is to devastate the credibility of the field of psychiatry in general and the expert's credibility in particular. Many useful techniques are provided in Jay Ziskin's *Coping with Psychiatric and Psychological Testimony*.[17] Ziskin, a lawyer as well as a psychologist, believes that psychiatric testimony does not belong in the courtroom. His goal is to see psychiatric testimony excluded because of its unreliability. This idea can be used in two ways. The first is by a legal argument to the court in a pretrial evidentiary hearing. If the prosecution is successful, all psychiatric evidence will be excluded from the trial. The argument to advance for this proposition is that psychiatric evidence is nothing more than mere speculation; that it is less reliable than polygraph examinations, and that it tends to confuse rather than clarify issues. If it is not a reliable tool in the search for truth, the testimony should not be admitted into evidence.

The problems with the pretrial hearing idea are that the prosecution loses the advantage of surprise if it loses at this stage of the proceeding. In addition, psychiatric testimony is commonly admitted, and an argument can be mounted that the legislature intended psychiatric testimony to be used in insanity cases.[18]

The second way to utilize the ambush method is to attack the field of psychiatry on cross-examination of the defendant's expert and on rebuttal. If the attack is launched correctly, it will have the added advantage of surprise, and the defendant's insanity case will be shattered. By this point in the trial, the defendant's insanity case will be difficult to salvage.

Notes

1. *State* v. *Elizabeth Nicholas*, Lane County (Oregon) Circuit Court No. 76-584.

2. *State* v. *Phillips*, 245 Or. 466, 422 P.2d 670 (1967).

3. *Shepard* v. *Bowe*, 250 Or. 288, 422 P.2d 238 (1968).

4. *State* v. *Whitlow*, 45 N.J. 3, 210 A.2d 763, (1965):767.

5. The Oregon Supreme Court reaffirmed *Shepard* v. *Bowe* in *State ex rel.* v. *Woodrich*, 279 Or. 31, 566 P.2d 859 (1977).

6. *State ex rel. Johnson* v. *Richardson*, 276 Or. 325, 555 P.2d 202 (1976). The questions the defendant must answer do not include those concerning his acts or conduct at or near the time of the alleged crime. See *Shepard* v. *Bowe*.

7. See *Lee* v. *County Court of Erie County*, 27 N.Y. 2d 432, 328 N.Y.S. 2d 705, 267 N.E. 2d 452, *cert. den.* 404 U.S. 974 (1971); *United States* v. *Albright*, 388 F.2d 719 (4th Cir., 1968); *United States* v. *Baird*, 414 F.2d 700 (1969); *State* v. *Whitlow*. In New Jersey, the jury is instructed that psychiatric evidence can be considered only on the issue of sanity and not on the issue of guilt. *State* v. *Whitlow*. However, in Oregon there is no rule to prevent the state from introducing evidence derived from psychiatric interviews as proof that the defendant committed the crime. There is no psychiatrist-patient privilege in Oregon. See Oregon Revised Statutes 44.040.

8. *State* v. *Roger Dyke*, Land County (Oregon) Circuit Court No. 74-298.

9. Currently in Oregon, the defendant is presumed sane, and the defense must prove insanity by a preponderance of the evidence. See *State* v. *Butchek*, 121 Or. 141, 154, 253 P.367 (1927).

10. *Leland* v. *Oregon*, 343 U.S. 790 (1952).

11. *Mullaney* v. *Wilbur*, 44 L.E.d 508 (1975).

12. The state of Oregon, for example, defines extreme emotional disturbances in subsection 2 of ORS 163.115: "For the purpose of paragraph (a) of subsection (1) of this section, a homicide which would otherwise be murder is committed under the influence of extreme emotional disturbance when such disturbance is not the result of the person's own intentional, knowing, reckless or criminally negligent act, and for which disturbance there is a reasonable explanation. The reasonableness of the explanation for the disturbance shall be determined from the standpoint of an ordinary person in the actor's situation under the circumstances as the actor reasonably believes them to be." See *State* v. *McCoy*, 17 Or. App. 155, 521 P.2d 1074 (1974), where the Oregon Court of Appeals held that the state has the burden of negating the element of extreme emotional disturbance in a murder prosecution.

13. See California Penal Code, sec. 1026 for bifurcated trial procedure.

14. A. Goldstein, A. Dershowitz, and R. Schwartz, *Criminal Law: Theory and Process* (New York: Free Press, 1979), p. 1115.

15. The Oregon legislature codified this rule in ORS 41.900(2) and ORS 41.900(3). The U.S. Congress codified it in the Federal Rules of Evidence, rule 804(1).

16. See ORS 44.040(d).

17. J. Ziskin, *Coping with Psychiatric and Psychological Testimony* (Beverly Hills: Law and Psychology Press, 1970).

18. *State* v. *Dyer*, 16 App. 247 (1974), p. 258.

4

Beginning the Trial

Voir dire, one of the tactically critical phases of a trial, is the first opportunity to influence the jurors for or against the defense of insanity. By setting the stage in voir dire, the prosecutor can take an early advantage in combating the insanity bid. Just as in any other trial, the prosecutor should be positive and firm in this phase, communicating an air of confidence and leadership to the jury. One of his primary goals is to make the jury aware that the prosecution represents the people of the county in the trial. If he is successful, he will have provided a common denominator between prosecutor and jury, and the jurors now should look to him for direction. The next step is to inform the jurors about the insanity defense. Initially the prosecutor should change the terminology. Rather than asking questions couched in terms of insanity, he is advised to use terms like *responsibility* and *accountability*. For example, the Oregon statute says that "a person is not responsible for criminal conduct if . . ."[1] Therefore the basis for using the word *responsibility* instead of *insanity* is found in the law. In fact the law does not use words like *insane* or *crazy* and the jury should be deflected from such terms because of their connotations. To the average person the ability to commit a detestable crime connotes insanity or derangement. However, the prosecution must point out to the jurors that although the defendant's behavior may not seem rational to them, it is logical for the criminal or criminally minded. This distinction is important. Psychiatrists will testify that no one person is normal; instead there is a wide range of behavior called normal, and deviations are not necessarily abnormal. To possess a criminal mind is not to be insane. Questions regarding this distinction are important as a foundation to be tied to closing argument. The prosecution should ask the jurors if they believe that all criminals are insane:

Do you, Mr. Juror, feel that all criminals are mentally ill?

Do you understand that under our law, people who have a propensity to commit crimes are not mentally ill just because they keep committing crimes?[2]

Now, if the state proves that this defendant committed a horrible crime that you or I wouldn't do, will that fact alone make you think that he has a mental problem for which the law provides an excuse?

31

> If the state proves that the defendant committed a detestable crime, and the defendant hasn't proven to you that he has a mental disease for which the law will excuse him, will you be able to uphold the law and convict him of the crime charged in the indictment?

Questions of this nature will provide to the prosecution the opportunity in closing argument to go back and tell the jury that each one promised that they could differentiate between a criminal mind and a mentally diseased one and that they promised they would uphold the law and find the defendant guilty if the state met its burden and the defense did not prove that the defendant lacked criminal responsibility at the time he committed the crime.

It is important to clarify the issue in terms most favorable to the state, though there may be some question as to how far the prosecutor may proceed in this area. If the defendant is basically conceding the case on the facts, a question may be thus phrased, "Do you understand, Mr. Juror, that what we are trying to determine here is whether the state has the right to hold this defendant responsible for a terrible crime?" If the defendant is riding the two-horse theory—that he did not commit the crime but if he did he is crazy—the question must be phrased somewhat differently: "Do you understand, Mr. Juror, that we must solve two mysteries in this trial: did the defendant commit this horrible act, and if he did, does the state have the right to hold him accountable?"

The prosecutor should bring up the point that the insanity defense may be abused in our criminal-justice system:

> Do you, Mr. Juror, understand that the plea of not guilty by reason of insanity is a legitimate plea? Do you understand that it is provided for by law? Now we don't know very much about you folks on the jury panel, and that is why we're asking these questions. There are some people who would say that the insanity plea is an overworked and abused device in our criminal law, one that is used by those charged with major crimes in an attempt to "beat the rap." Is there anyone here that feels that way?

Probably no one will say yes, though it has happened. In the *State* v. *Robert Armstrong*, some jurors felt that a person should always be held responsible for his acts. Those jurors were dismissed, but the prosecution benefited from their remarks because they represented strong views from objective nonpartisan citizens. These views were initiated independently of the prosecution, but they were identical in spirit, and they helped to unify the prosecution with the jury.[3] To further this development, the prosecution may want to phrase its questions in the following manner: "Mr. Juror, before you *set the defendant free* of criminal responsibility, . . ."

It is important to devote some general questioning to the field of expert witnesses. It may be crucial to impress upon the jurors the idea that expert witnesses are the same as regular witnesses except that they are supposed to have expertise in a particular area of knowledge. The prosecution should point out that opposing psychiatrists usually review the same evidence and may reach opposite conclusions. Establishing this fact will help point out the nebulous nature of the art. The prosecutor may want to ask the jurors if any of them has come in contact with a psychiatrist or knows anyone who has required his services. If the juror reports that the psychiatrist (or psychologist) had a positive effect, the prosecutor may want to challenge. A juror who sympathizes with psychiatrists is not a person whom the prosecutor wants examining antipsychiatric evidence. On the other hand, questioning of this sort may identify jurors who can relate negative experiences with psychiatrists, thus influencing the rest of the jurors. A prosecutor who wants to hear a juror speak should ask an abstract question such as, "do you think psychiatry is a science or an art?" Some jurors may not understand the question, and others will not know how to react, but those who do will reveal their feelings. It will be important to let the jury know that psychiatrists will differ; that the defense has the burden of proof, and that if the defense does not meet its burden, the state wins. A prosecutor using either the ambush or bullet methods probably should request that all nurses, doctors, or other health professionals be dismissed from the jury panel.

In every case, the defense lawyer will talk about the presumption of innocence and proving the case beyond a reasonable doubt. However, a prosecutor who can bring up these points before the defense does can take the wind out of the defendant's sails. A prosecutor who gives the jury the impression that the state wants to play fair in the end will be the only one who looks as if he is playing fair. He should ask the jurors if they understand that the defendant is presumed innocent, that the grand-jury indictment is not to be regarded as evidence of guilt, and that the state has the burden of proving guilt beyond a reasonable doubt. The jury should be told that this burden is one that the state readily accepts because the trial process is a search for the truth, the state's purpose. It is a good idea for the prosecutor to emphasize the respective burdens of proof with a question such as this one: "You realize that I must prove the defendant guilty of the act alleged in the indictment. And if I don't you should find the defendant not guilty. And just as you are going to require me to prove the state's case, will you require the defendant to prove that he should not be held responsible for his crime?" The following line of questioning is also useful:

> Now, we don't know what the defense is going to be in this case. The defendant has filed notice of mental disease or defect in this case, but we don't know if he's saying he didn't do it, or if he's saying he did do it, but he's not responsible. You will recognize, won't you, that it can't be both ways? If he says he didn't do it, then there's no reason to say that he should be found to be not responsible for something he didn't do, right?

The closing argument can contain words to this effect: "Counsel in this trial is paid by the defendant to do one thing: To prevent the defendant from being found guilty. He has done a fine job, but remember what his job is—it is to see that this defendant walks out of here a free man. Now do you remember what I asked each of you before the trial? I asked if you realized that this trial was a search for the truth of this crime. I told you that this is what the state was after, the truth. Now I ask you, has Mr. Defense Counsel been concerned with the truth, or has he been solely preoccupied with getting his client off?" Phraseology of this sort will let the jury view the prosecutor as the protector of the truth-determining process.

During the case, the defense will put on only that evidence showing the defendant's abnormal mental condition. Usually this will include the defense psychiatrist and lay witnesses such as the defendant's parents or other relatives or friends who will relate experiences that could be construed as crazy behavior by the defendant. A prosecutor who puts on rebuttal evidence showing the defendant's normal behavior or that he was just an antisocial criminal can legitimately claim in final argument that the defendant was not really interested in showing the jury the whole truth. This prosecutor can point out that he has attempted to show them both sides.

Just as in the other phases of the trial, the extent of the prosecutor's actions will depend on where and how far the defense attorney goes. If in voir dire the defense develops the expected evidence, the prosecutor will want to respond accordingly. In fact, this may present an opportunity to begin the process of persuading the jury toward the state's point of view. For example, in a brutal murder case, the prosecutor can combine his explanation of the defendant's deeds with the observation that just because the defendant brutally killed the victim, he should not be excused from responsibility; otherwise all other such murderers would be excused.

In voir dire the jurors also should be asked if they have any personal or religious beliefs or philosophies that would prevent them from reaching a guilty verdict if the state does prove its case and the defendant does not establish his defense.

After the jurors have been posed hypothetical problems peripherally concerning the prosecution's case, it is time to start unraveling the mystery created during voir dire. The jurors have been informed that the defendant has filed notice of mental disease or defect, and they have been read the indictment. The prosecutor's task now is to depict the defendant as committing the deed in a cold, clear-thinking manner. (Some jurisdictions require the prosecutor to state a prima-facie case during his opening statement. In those jurisdictions, a motion to dismiss will be granted if the prosecutor does not state such a case in opening, and no evidence will be heard.)[4] He should outline the proof he will offer on each element of the crime charged, paying particular attention to the culpable mental state. It is a good idea for him to list all of the facts in the case that tend to show that the defendant was aware of his actions. These facts should be revealed to the jury in his opening statement. Even if all of these facts are not emphasized in the trial, the jury will be aware of them and will independently pick up on some of them as the trial progresses.

The prosecution has the advantage of striking first, and it should seize upon the opportunity to give a detailed and hard-hitting account of what the evidence will prove. By providing the jury with a detailed preview, the prosecutor makes his job easier in closing because the jury will know how the evidence fits in as they hear it. He should not make the mistake of assuming that the jury will absorb all of the pertinent points he expects to bring out in evidence. Clarence Darrow once described the jury as "twelve men of average ignorance." Another advantage of the detailed-account approach is that if the evidence proves what he told the jury that it would, he has fulfilled his part of a contract. The jury will then trust and respect him.

If the defendant has a strong insanity case, the prosecutor should talk about psychiatric testimony in his opening statement. He should tell the jury that he anticipates psychiatric testimony to be produced by the defendant, and that if that is the case, the state will be presenting expert testimony as well. He should also emphasize that the jury may find the defendant strange but that he is still legally responsible for his crime. A prosecutor who is using the bullet or ambush methods may want to make a few negative remarks about psychiatric testimony.

The facts of the case should be presented as the path to the resolution of the issues. American legal theory is founded upon the Judeo-Christian ethic. The key principle from this tradition in respect to the criminal-justice system is that everyone is personally and individually responsible for their deeds. Under this ethic, a person who commits a crime has made a choice, an act of his own free will, and he should be held accountable for that act. Most Americans accept this concept, so it will be a powerful one that deserves emphasis at every opportunity. The opening statement should point to the facts rather than get immersed in psychiatric terminology.

The conclusion to the statement should assert that the state does not know exactly what the defense is, but that it will be an attempt to excuse the defendant's conduct by way of some kind of mental theory. The jurors' attention should be directed to the facts, because the facts will establish that the defendant was aware of what he was doing.

Notes

1. Oregon Revised Statutes 161.295.
2. Some statutes, such as Oregon's (ORS 161.295(2)), exclude

sociopaths from the defense of lack of responsibility due to mental disease or defect.

3. *State* v. *Robert Armstrong*, 38 Or. App. 219, 589 P.2d 1174 (1979).

4. In Oregon and other jurisdictions, it is not necessary to cover every element of the crime charged because the opening statement is not considered to be a pleading but rather an opportunity for counsel to outline to the jury the evidence the party plans to introduce, and its relevance to the issues. See *State* v. *Keaton*, 15 Or. App. 477 (1973), and *State* v. *Reynolds*, 164 Or. 446 (1940). If the facts do not establish that the defendant knew what he was doing if the crime is incomprehensible, and if the state cannot find a psychiatrist who can testify for it, it may be advisable not to go to trial. Not every mental defense can be defeated. The key to success is to avoid being at the mercy of the psychiatrists, who very often want to find an excuse for the defendant's conduct.

5 The Credentials Game

A fundamental belief in our system of law has been that each person is accountable for his own deeds. In the late 1960s, however, this concept was attacked and a new one, which we call the *society-did-it doctrine*, emerged, in which numerous reasons were espoused as justification for crime. Psychiatrists and psychologists were among the primary proponents of this concept. As a result, during the time that this movement enjoyed its highest popularity, they were viewed in an important light. The reasoning behind this is understandable. By putting the blame on society for criminal episodes and in so doing exculpating the criminal, the American consciousness could realistically believe that all people are essentially good. Thus crime occurs as the result of some societal malfunctioning or injustice. Since people are basically good, crime will disappear when the malfunctioning is eliminated. Psychiatrists were there to provide the answers.[1] Although this concept has lost popularity, psychiatrists still enjoy the high esteem of the public, and this is an obstacle to attorneys (who perhaps do not enjoy that same respect) in cross-examining psychiatrists. Therefore it is tactically important to deflate that balloon in an examination of the expert's credentials.

Three major areas are subject to attack in this regard: the psychiatrist's education, his experience, and the strength of his knowledge of the particular discipline. The purpose of the credentials game is to expose the deficiencies of the psychiatrist's education, to point out unsettled areas of psychiatric knowledge, and to have the jury hear from the psychiatrist himself that his field involves a high degree of fallibility.

The best approach is to question the expert's credentials directly after opposing counsel has sought to qualify the witness as an expert. These questions generally are asked in aid of an objection, but the trial court may be unwilling to allow this. The rule in Oregon is that a party does not have the absolute right to question an opposing expert witness's qualifications before the witness is entitled to express his opinion. However, the trial court in its discretion may permit the prosecutor to pursue this line of questioning before the expert delivers his opinion. In an Oregon case, the court suggested:

> If no sufficient foundation is laid for opinion testimony, an objection may be made on that ground. A trial court may, "in aid of an objection," permit questions to be asked by opposing counsel relating to the qualifications of a witness or the foundation for his testimony. A trial court is not required

to do so, however, but may insist that all such questions be postponed until cross-examination. If it then appears that there is no proper basis for the testimony given on direct examination, a motion may be made to strike such testimony.[2]

Convincing the trial court to permit an examination of the expert's qualifications before he is allowed to state his opinion will accomplish two key tactical maneuvers. First, the jury will become aware from the prosecutor's questions and the expert's answers that there are serious deficiencies with respect to this so-called expert knowledge they are about to hear. They will then weigh more skeptically what they hear from the psychiatrist. Second, the expert will realize that the prosecution knows something about the vagueness and deficiencies of psychiatry and will be listening carefully to his testimony. His composure may be a bit shaken in the knowledge that he may be questioned closely at any time.

The first line of questioning should concern the expert's academic degrees. At this point, the defense has let the expert tell the jury about his academic background. Now the prosecutor must explain to the jury that during the expert's eight to ten years of college and professional school, probably fewer than two years were spent learning about psychiatry. (No time in undergraduate work and only a brief period in medical school is spent on formal psychiatric training.)[3] Additionally the American Board of Psychiatry and Neurology does not even require two years of psychiatric experience for certification. A report in the *American Journal of Psychiatry* claims that psychiatrists protect themselves by substituting medical or surgical training for psychiatric experience:

> . . . a person with two years of training in colon and rectal surgery may count this as a year of experience in psychiatry. In contrast, a person who has had two years experience as a Ph.D. clinical psychologist cannot receive credit because psychology is not a medical specialty.[4]

The next step for the prosecutor is to ask the psychiatrist how much of his professional education was actually relevant to the study of psychiatry.

Several questions relating to the expert's practical experience can be useful: "Doctor, how long have you been engaged in the practice of psychiatry? During that time how may evaluations have you made based on psychiatric interviews? What kinds of follow-ups, empirical studies, have you performed on your patients to determine the reliability of your initial diagnosis?" The common answer to this last question is none. Following this answer, the doctor should be asked why he can support his conclusions based upon experience, since he may have been wrong more than right.

Another area of inquiry is the substance behind the psychiatrist's title. The psychiatrist probably will have pointed out that he is board certified. (If the expert is not board certified, this should be mentioned to the jury.) Psychiatrists must pass the Psychiatry National Board Examination to be certified. But one study has concluded that a college freshman can usually pass the written part of the board examination with very little preparation.[5]

After the deficiencies in the psychiatrist's education, experience, and the certification process have been revealed, one or two avenues of attack are left with respect to the expert's credentials. Professor James V. McConnell has suggested two approaches.

First, no one can know everything. In fact, for an individual to be infallible, he must know everything and know it well. It is not difficult to find some areas that an expert does not know but should. It is the job of the prosecutor to find these gaps and demonstrate a flaw in the expert's knowledge. One way to keep current is to read one of the better medical journals, such as *Medical World News* or the *New England Journal of Medicine*. McConnell suggests that just before trial, the prosecutor should locate an experiment or survey that is at least tangentially related to the topic about which the expert will testify. With that information in hand, the prosecutor is prepared to confront the expert. In questioning, the prosecutor should let the expert commit himself on a specific point and then ask if this new research has any bearing on the issues. Probably the expert will not have read the article because it is too recent, and he will try to evade the context of the question. And even if he is familiar with the article, he still must accept the findings and insist that they support his position or reject the findings as inaccurate or inappropriate. McConnell notes, "Whether he accepts or rejects the . . . findings, all you have to do is to nod sagely and mutter, 'Yes, indeed, Doctor, I rather thought you'd take that position,' shake your head, shrug your shoulders, and turn away from him slowly."[6]

McConnell's second suggestion is called the primary-source gambit. The expert will be testifying to facts derived basically from textbooks and other secondary-source material. Yet being an expert should require more. This is particularly true if the expert witness views himself as a scientist because scientists are expected to do original research and to read and review the original research of others. McConnell suggests that prosecutors utilize the criticisms of secondary analysis to their advantage in the courtroom. The approach is to wait for the expert to make a statement about something he could not have seen take place, and then ask him how he knows about it, who discovered it, and where it was first published. Once the expert has answered those questions, he can be asked how long ago he read the original research. Probably he has never seen the original piece. Once he admits to that, he should be asked if this is such an important point that it should be read in the original. This method will destroy part of his credibility. If he insists that secondary sources are appropriate, the prosecutor can ask if he has ever noted mistakes in textbooks he has read and should be sure to have examples of mistakes (which are easily found).

No matter what the expert has said previously, the prosecutor should get him to admit that he owes it to the jury, the court, and the defendant to have gone straight to the original source because a secondary interpretation may reveal a mistake in interpretation. Once the expert admits that he has not read a certain primary source, he can be challenged on every factual statement he makes, wanting to know about the original research publication. McConnell concludes that "such a tactic, if well handled should convince the jury that you don't really trust this man's expertise."[7]

McConnell's suggestions are good ones that can be applied easily in court. For example, in a recent mental-defense case, McConnell's method was used and provided effective results. In *State* v. *Ronald Reynolds*, the defendant was charged with strong-arm robbery and assault. The victim picked up the defendant who was hitch-hiking, took him to a motel room, and allegedly made homosexual advances toward him. The defendant beat the victim, bound and gagged him, and left the motel with most of his possessions, including a large sum of money and a late-model car. The state's theory was that the defendant was a classic example of an antisocial person. The defense claimed that the defendant had a mental defect based upon homosexual panic. In order to establish this defense, a psychologist testified on the basis of Rorschach tests that the defendant had problems with his own sexual identity.[8]

Using McConnell's methodology, the prosecutor researched literature on the psychology of sexual behavior and discovered an empirical study discussing many of the issues involved in this case.[9] On cross-examination, the psychologist was asked questions that this research addressed. He was asked specifically if he had read this particular article. He had not but hedged around the question. He was next asked whether the article was useful in considering homosexuality and potential responses to it. It was at this point that the psychologist made his error. He had not read the article and, in fact, had never heard of it. Instead of admitting his ignorance, he pretended to know the material and suggested it was useless. When asked how he could testify that a study was useless when he had not read it, he responded that it was not necessary to have read all of the research on a particular topic. He was asked several questions about the type of study that was mentioned, and he answered them in such a fashion that his credibility was severely damaged and his composure was shaken. Although the jury had many issues to consider in this trial, they rejected unanimously the mental defense and returned a verdict of guilty after only one-half hour of deliberation.

Many other techniques can be used against the expert in this phase of questioning. If the prosecution is allowed to question the expert's credentials before he is allowed to express an opinion, it will be in a tactically advantageous position. A word of caution: The trial judge probably will permit only a limited number of questions, so the prosecutor should choose them carefully to fit the particular situation best.

Notes

1. N. Caplan and S. Nelson, "On Being Useful," *American Psychologist* 28 (March 1973):199-211.

2. *Krause* v. *Eugene Dodge*, 265 Or. 486, 509, 510 P.2d 1199 (1973).

3. The expert might be asked to list all of the courses he took in medical school dealing with thought, emotion, learning, perception, and behavioral adaptation. This is psychological training and would seem necessary to a psychiatrist, yet the study of psychology is virtually ignored in medical school.

4. R.L. Taylor and E. Tarney, "Pseudo Regulation of American Psychiatry," *American Journal of Psychiatry* 129 (1972):659.

5. C.M. Pierce, J. Mathias, and U. Pishkin, "Basic Psychiatry in Twelve Hours," *Diseases of the Nervous System* 29 (1968):533-535.

6. James McConnell, "Doctors are People Too," *Michigan State Bar Journal* 47 (October 1968):21.

7. Ibid., p. 23.

8. *State* v. *Ronald Reynolds*, Lane County (Oregon) Circuit Court Case 10-80-03434.

9. L.J. Chapman and Jean Chapman, "Test Results Are What You Think They Are," *Psychology Today* 5 (November 1971):18-22, 106-107. This article asserted that clinicians often determined signs of homosexuality based on interpretations of cards 4 and 6 of the Rorschach tests, although there is no validation to back them up. The Chapmans do not criticize the Rorschach tests, only the way they are used by clinicians.

6 The Myth about Psychological Testing

The devices that are most widely used in an insanity-based defense are psychological tests. These tests are used primarily to bolster the psychiatrist's (or psychologist's) opinion by providing an authoritative foundation upon which the doctor can rely to support his position. These diagnostic tests also can be used to contradict and impeach an adverse expert's opinion. A basic understanding of the relative strengths and weaknesses of these tests can supply the attorney with an ability to confuse an expert's opinion since the very nature of the tests themselves rests upon a foundation without substance.

The first question to be addressed about a particular test concerns for whom it was designed. The second is to what group of people this test was first given (that is, upon what group the norm was derived?). Invariably the answer will not include a group of criminal defendants. This concept is very important because if the test was not designed for criminal defendants, many conflicting factors are interjected into the situation that the test was not designed to measure. For example, if the norm is a group of patients who have nothing to gain by being evasive, or if the group has nothing to gain by appearing demented, the test may not be able to deal with criminal defendants who may, in fact, have very much to gain by being untruthful. Furthermore, the normal testing situation may call for a given set of conditions, essential in any empirical method, and a jail may not conform with the required test environment. In addition, the subject may truthfully answer questions in a jail, hospital, or other institutionally controlled environment that indicate only a very natural fear; whereas the same answers in an uncontrolled environment may indicate extreme paranoia. This is particularly prevalent in the Minnesota Multi-Phasic Personality Inventory (MMPI), which is now normally scored by a computer and makes no distinction between responses from individuals in controlled as opposed to uncontrolled environments.

It is essential to address these fundamental questions to the expert witness about each test used:

1. For whom was this test originally designed?
2. From what group was the norm derived?
3. When was this test last updated?
4. Does this test include a truth scale?

5. If not, how does one determine if a person is lying or malingering?
6. Quantitatively, what is the reliability of this test?
7. Does this test distinguish between individuals who are incarcerated as opposed to individuals living in an uncontrolled environment?
8. Are the results of this test subject to different interpretations?
9. Under what conditions was the test designed to be administered? Were the conditions similar in this case? If not, how are the results affected?
10. Doctor, to how many patients have you given this test?
11. How many of them has the test shown to be problem free?
12. Don't you think that this test has an inherent bias toward showing a person to be problem-ridden?
13. What is the coefficient of reliability that your colleagues attach to this test?
14. Have you read the latest article evaluating this test? [The prosecution should have read by indexing the *Annual Review of Psychology*, *Psychological Abstracts*, or *Mental Measurement Yearbook*. Probably the doctor will not have read this article, which makes a bad impression on the jury. Even if he has, the prosecution can point out the current criticism of the test, which the doctor will be forced to acknowledge.]
15. What is this test designed to measure?
16. Do you as a psychiatrist sometimes reach a conclusion different than that suggested by a psychological test? [He will answer yes.]
17. Upon which do you then rely: your clinical judgment or the test? [Psychiatrists will always, and psychologists will usually, reject the tests if they do not correlate with the doctor's clinical judgment.]

Minnesota Multi-Phasic Personality Inventory

The most commonly used psychological test is the objective Minnesota Multi-Phasic Personality Inventory (MMPI), which was designed in 1940 and last updated in 1970. It consists of 550 statements that the test subject is asked to respond to by marking true or false on an answer sheet. The answer sheets are generally sent to a computer center, where they are tabulated by computer and then returned to the psychologist. (Some psychologists still tabulate the tests themselves.) The computer tabulates the answers and returns an evaluation printout.

The MMPI was first given to a hospital population and seven hundred visitors of University of Minnesota hospitals (these visitors represented the normal control group). According to Anastasi, this represented an adequate sampling of the Minnesota population of both sexes, ages sixteen to fifty-five.[1]

Lawyers should immediately recognize inherent problems with the MMPI. What difference could it make that the normal control group was an adequate sampling of Minnesota's population? What is the ethnic background of Minnesota? Is it comparable to the national ethnic makeup? To a particular state's ethnic makeup? Furthermore, of what use is a computer printout? What information is fed into the computer banks? Is background information about the defendant fed into the computer? (It is not.) Does the computer make distinctions for patients in uncontrolled, as opposed to controlled, environments? (It does not.) Can a computer without background information about a patient, with no knowledge of his environment, with a faulty and inaccurate normal control group (unrelated to your defendant), adequately analyze this person's personality makeup? (It cannot.)

The MMPI consists of many different scales. The following list represents the standard scales used (besides the validity scales) in the MMPI, with a brief definition of what each seeks to diagnose:

1. Hs (hypochondriasis): The affliction of imaginary illnesses.
2. D (depression): Measures psychotic or neurotic melancholia.
3. Hy (hysteria): A neurosis (psychoneurosis) that assumes protean forms, such as anesthesias, disassociations, paralyses, and other functional disorders; in psychoanalysis (early Freud), the representation of unconscious, repressed fantasies or (later Freud) the result of a breakdown of defenses against unconscious anxieties.
4. Pd (psychopathic deviate): *Psychopath* is a loose term denoting an antisocial or hostile individual.
5. Mf (masculinity-feminity): High scores on this test indicate similarities with the opposite sex. The scale has been used frequently to determine homosexuality.
6. Pa (paranoia): A condition in which systematized delusions that are often internally consistent are present in an individual.
7. Pt (psychasthenia): A neurotic disorder characterized by phobias, loss of psychic energy, obsessions and compulsions, tics, and anxieties.
8. Sc (schizophrenia): A severe mental disorder characterized by loss of contact with reality and profound behavioral maladjustments.
9. Ma (hypomania): A slight degree of excitement. In a manic-depressive disorder, manic type, great emotional tensions occur, and this scale denotes their presence. However, these tensions are less than those occurring in acute and in hyperacute mania.[2]

The MMPI has some very specific and fundamental flaws. The first indication that the MMPI cannot diagnose a person as problem-free appears in the first paragraph of instructions: "The questions you are about to answer are designed to help you tell about your attitudes, feelings and *problems*. They will provide additional information for making decisions about your *treatment*."[3] The significant words here are *problems* and *treatment*. In the context of the paragraph, there is a presumption that the test-taker has a problem and the test is designed to prescribe treatment. Indeed the computer readout will suggest a treatment, and for that reason alone should be inadmissible, because in prescribing treatment, sentencing is suggested. This presumption that the test-taker has problems should invalidate the test as a courtroom exhibit, for if a test is designed to find existing problems, the same test cannot be used to determine whether a person has a problem in the first place. Indeed there is the suggestion that without prior evidence of a mental or emotional problem, the automated MMPI should not be given to a criminal defendant:

> The interpretation system was developed for use with patients who are in difficulty or distress because of disturbances in their behavior or emotional state. It is designed specifically for patients seen in clinical practice and at hospitals and clinics. *IT IS NOT SUITABLE FOR ROUTINE SCREENING OF PRESUMABLY NORMAL-RANGE INDIVIDUALS.*[4]

It may be argued that a criminal defendant may be in a clinical position and the test given for a clinical purpose. But if the defendant has no history of mental or emotional problems, the MMPI should not be given. If the rationale is that the defendant allegedly committed a crime and therefore has a behavioral problem and should be given the test, we could easily end up with the conclusion that all criminals must be crazy. Since this is not the accepted viewpoint, the logical conclusion is that before a defendant should be given the MMPI, there must be other evidence of mental or emotional problems. If the defense psychiatrist launches his diagnosis by relying on the MMPI, this claim can be disputed by the charge that it is based on a foundation without substance and that the doctor violated the guidelines of his profession in relation to administering the MMPI prematurely. If the MMPI has been administered and the court rules that the psychiatrist or psychologist can testify about the results, the prosecutor will still have the opportunity to impeach the content of the test.

Perhaps the most valid criticism of using the MMPI in the courtroom can be made when the test is administered to a defendant who is in custody. The reason is that almost 20 percent of the questions on it are inappropriate to give a person who is in custody. Consider the following.

3. I wake up fresh and rested most mornings.
4. I wish I could be as happy as others seem to be.
70. I believe I am being plotted against.
86. I certainly feel useless at times.
92. Most nights I go to sleep without thoughts or ideas bothering me.

It would be very rare for someone to wake up fresh and rested most mornings in jail. It is also to be presumed that people are not happy in jail, feel useless at times, and are troubled by upcoming trials in which police and prosecutors are plotting against them. So a defendant in jail who answered these questions truthfully would be responding normally to the negative stimuli of a jail cell. But since the automated test makes no provision for the defendant in jail, the computer readout is apt to project that this person is a manic-depressive with paranoid overtones. Additionally since the likelihood is that the MMPI will be given to a defendant several months after the crime and several months after the defendant has been in jail, the test will tell nothing about the defendant's state of mind at the time of the act but rather how he responds to a prison cell.

In the case of *State* v. *Robert Armstrong*, the defendant was charged with murdering a grocery-store clerk during a holdup.[5] Armstrong had no history of mental disease or defect, although he showed propensities toward sociopathic conduct. Since the facts were conclusive, he interposed an insanity defense. Armstrong was given the MMPI after he spent forty-five days in jail. Below is a list of thirty-eight critical items and Armstrong's responses to them:

70. I believe I am being plotted against. (False.)
72. I believe I am being followed. (False.)
424. Someone has been trying to poison me. (False.)
306. There are persons who are trying to steal my thoughts and ideas. (False.)
152. Someone has control over my mind. (False.)
147. At one or more times in my life I felt that someone was making me do things by hypnotizing me. (False.)
159. Someone has been trying to influence my mind. (False).
17. Evil spirits possess me at times. (False.)
30. When I am with people I am bothered by hearing very queer things. (False).
40. I see things or animals or people around me that others do not see. (False.)
102. There is something wrong with my mind. (False.)
109. I am afraid of losing my mind. (True.)
110. I commonly hear voices without knowing where they come from. (False.)
178. Peculiar odors come to me at times. (True.)
187. I often feel as if things were not real. (True.)
189. I have strange and peculiar thoughts. (True.)
423. I hear strange things when I am alone. (True.)
21. I have had very peculiar and strange experiences. (No answer.)
12. My sex life is satisfactory. (True.)
173. I have never been in trouble because of my sex behavior. (True.)
43. I am very strongly attracted by members of my own sex. (True.)

45. I have often wished I were a girl. (False.)
79. I have never indulged in any unusual sex practices. (True.)
177. I am worried about sex matters. (False).
285. I have the wanderlust and am never happy unless I am roaming or traveling about. (False.)
94. I have had periods in which I carried on activities without knowing later what I had been doing. (True.)
122. At times it has been impossible for me to keep from stealing or shoplifting something. (True.)
226. I have used alcohol excessively. (True.)
120. I believe I am a condemned person. (False.)
311 I believe my sins are unpardonable. (True.)
182. Most of the time I wish I were dead. (False.).
394. I am afraid of using a knife or anything very sharp or pointed. (False.)
27. Much of the time my head seems to hurt all over. (True.)
261. Sometimes I am strongly attracted by the personal articles of others such as shoes, gloves, etc., so that I want to handle or steal them though I have no use for them. (False.)
68. Often I feel as if there were a tight band about my head. (True.)
84. Sometimes I feel as if I must injure either myself or some one else. (True.)
145. I have had blank spells in which my activities were interrupted and I did not know what was going on around me. (True.)
180. I feel anxiety about something or someone almost all the time. (False.)[6]

Almost all of these items should not be given to a person in jail because they permit the automated readout to diagnose a personality defect, when a prisoner might only be reacting normally to jail conditions. Armstrong did not give very many unusual responses, but the computer readout noted several:

Unusual Thoughts and Experiences

a.   I am afraid of losing my mind. (True.)
b.   Peculiar odors come to me at times. (True.)
c.   I cannot keep my mind on one thing. (True.)
d.   I have strange and peculiar thoughts. (True.)

These are not strange responses for a person who has just committed murder. Since Armstrong decided to plead insanity, the response to item a is not unusual. There were peculiar odors in the jail in which he was incarcerated (item b). No matter what one thinks about if he has recently murdered, he will, if he is normal, always be haunted by the act (item c). Considering Armstrong's predicament, strange thoughts are hardly inappropriate (item d).

Depression, Guilt, and Self-Destructive Ideas

    a.   I wish I could be as happy as others seem to be. (True.)
    b.   Most of the time I feel blue. (True.)
    c.   Much of the time I feel as if I have done something wrong or evil. (True.)
    d.   I certainly feel useless at times. (True.)
    e.   Most nights I go to sleep without thoughts or ideas bothering me. (False.)
    f.   At times I think I am no good at all. (True.)
    g.   I worry quite a bit over possible misfortunes. (True.)

It is easy to see that Armstrong's responses to these questions are normal. He is naturally unhappy because he is in jail (items a and d). He feels he is no good and has done something wrong (items c and f) because he had murdered a grocery clerk. He is bothered at night about possible misfortunes, such as a life sentence (items e and g).

These statements were delineated in the computer printout because "they might denote problem areas, symptoms or experiences which would merit further explanation in subsequent interview." And yet considering the circumstances (and the computer did not), there is nothing unusual about these responses. Indeed the lack of these reactions would be most unusual.

The computer evaluation also includes the MMPI profile of the patient, as well as an explanation for each of the clinical scales. Figure 6-1 presents Armstrong's profile. Scores between 50 and 70 are within a normal range. Scores above 70 allegedly indicate potential pathology.

Validity Scales

The four scales to the left of the dotted line in figure 6-1 are the validity scales. This unique feature of the MMPI is designed principally to determine if the patient is lying, has a distorted self-image, or does not understand the test. The "?" or "cannot say" scale is designed to measure the number of questions left unanswered. High scores are supposed to indicate a lack of cooperation or indecision. High scores may also indicate deficient reading abilities. If more than thirty items are not answered, the test is returned to the patient, and the patient is requested to try harder. Yet a high score may also indicate that some of the questions may be ambiguous. The computer, however, is not equipped to handle this possibility. Question 322, "I like to talk about sex," is a good example. The question is stated in an absolute form. Most people probably cannot answer this question "yes" or "no," and "sometimes" might be the best answer. Yet "sometimes" is not allowed as an answer on the MMPI.

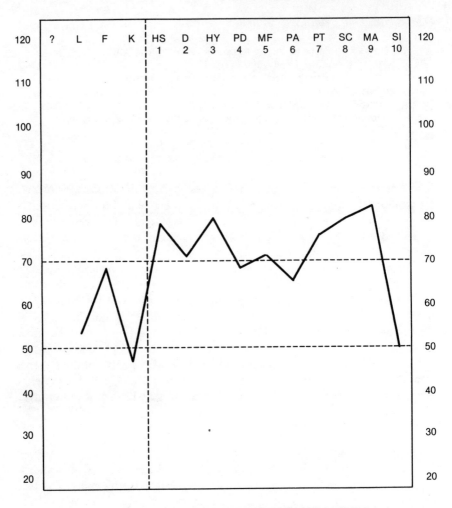

Figure 6-1. Bobby Armstrong: MMPI Profile

The L scale, which consists of fifteen items, is a self-image analysis. It is made up of minor faults that almost everyone has and to which most people would admit. A high score shows that the test-taker is overzealous in describing his attributes, while a low score suggests that a person is cognizant of his own faults and has no reservations about disclosing them.

The F scale is frequently referred to as the truth scale. But it is inaccurate if used exclusively. All four of the validity scales represent the truth factor of the test. The F scale is one of the largest portions of the test (sixty-four items). If the defendant scores over 80, the test is invalidated because the defendant was unable to read or understand the test items or made errors in filling out the answer sheet; was seriously confused, disorganized, or delusional; attempted to make himself look extremely disturbed; or did not cooperate and purposely responded in a random or irrelevant manner.[7] Low F scores indicate cooperation and comprehension. In an insanity defense, the prosecutor may persuasively argue that a high F score indicates that the defendant is attempting to make himself look bad. Armstrong's F score of 68 can be interpreted precisely in this manner. He pleaded insanity and knew that he had to appear insane to escape a murder conviction and a life sentence. Consequently a high F score resulted.

The final validity scale is the K scale (thirty items), designed to describe the test-taking attitudes and abilities of the patient. High scores indicate either defensiveness or contentment. Low scores show dissatisfaction and a propensity toward self-criticism.

Clinical Scales

Scale 1 (Hs). The Hs Scale denotes hypochondria (high score) and is designed to measure physical ailments: "Low Scale 1 scores suggest an ambitious, energetic, responsible person who is free from inhibitions and not overly concerned with physical complaints."[8] In Bobby Armstrong's case this hypochondria arguably may be attributed to the relatively unhealthy atmosphere of the jail or a willingness to show himself as abnormal. And yet the MMPI readout concluded differently:

> He is concerned, to an unusual degree, with bodily functions and health. He may overact to illnesses, and complain unreasonably about relatively minor aliments. Medical patients with this characteristic tend to be frustrating to their physicians because they complain of pains and disorders which are vague, difficult to identify, and may have no organic basis. Although some of these patients have a genuine physical illness, there is a strong psychological component, and they tend to be egocentric, demanding and pessimistic.

> In times of prolonged emotional stress he may develop psychophysiological symptoms such as headaches and gastrointestinal disorders. He appears to be a person who represses and denies emotional distress. While he may respond readily to advice and reassurance, he may be unwilling to accept a psychological interpretation of his difficulties.

Scale 2 (D). The depression scale is one of the more straightforward of the clinical scales. High scores indicate unhappiness and a negative outlook on life; low scores indicate cheerfulness and a positive outlook. A defendant, incarcerated or free, can be expected to score high on the depression scale because of the charges he faces. In the case of Armstrong, who scored 64 on the D scale (moderate to high), it is to be expected that if he is normal, he might regret killing a human being, be sorry about his predicament, and be worried about both his trial and his future. The readout confirms this interpretation:

> He is unhappy and discouraged, with a feeling that life is not working out well for him. He is filled with regrets and guilt about the past, and has little hope for the future. He often feels lonely, discouraged and misunderstood. His self-esteem is low, and he feels ineffectual and dissatisfied with himself.

Scale 3 (Hy). This scale measures conversion hysteria. Low scores indicate either a well-adjusted individual or a defensive, well-guarded person. High scores may indicate a propensity for acting out; in this case, the individual may be socially immature and emotionally unstable. High scores can also be interpreted to suggest a very weak individual, highly susceptible to suggestion. If a defendant scores high on this scale, the prosecutor can use this information to show how the score suggests very negative qualities about an individual but does not indicate any legitimate pathology.

Scale 4 (Pd). This scale is designed to measure a propensity to disregard social values (pathological deviant). For purposes of cross-examination, this can be categorized as the sociopathic scale. High scores indicate a tendency toward antisocial behavior, while moderate scores may indicate a healthy, adventurous life-style. Low scores may suggest that the patient cowers to authority.

Scale 5 (MF). The masculinity-femininity scale is used principally to determine overt similarities with the opposite sex. High scores for males indicate potential homosexuality; in females high scores indicate an aggressive masculine-oriented personality. Yet it is also possible to conclude that a high Mf score in a male indicates sensitivity, education, and a rich cultural background.

Low scores in males indicate an active, vigorous personality, and in females low scores indicate docility or traditional feminine interests.

Scale 6 (Pa). This paranoia scale may be the most inappropriate one in reference to criminal defendants in jail. It is designed to measure feelings of suspicion and persecution. The definition of paranoia is "a condition in which systematized delusions that are often internally consistent are present in an individual."[9] What may be a systematized delusion for one control group might be the reality for a prison population. This score is open to attack on this basis.

Scale 7 (Pt). The psychasthenia scale is designed to measure phobias, obsessions, and compulsions. High scores indicate excessive fears and anxieties, while low scores indicate a well-ordered and -organized personality. This scale, like scale 6, actually may indicate only a normal response to the fears and anxieties connected with waiting to be tried for a serious crime. For Bobby Armstrong, the printout stated:

> He is troubled by an unusual number of fears which tend to restrict his life, and make him uncomfortable in everyday activities. While the exact content of his fears would have to be elicited by interview, similar individuals have fears such as fire, spiders, heights, disease, closed places or storms. The wide variety of fears reported suggests a phobic reaction to chronic anxiety.

Armstrong, of course, was in jail awaiting trial for murder. Thus that he was "troubled by an unusual number of fears that tend to restrict his life, and make him uncomfortable in everyday activities" shows no evidence of pathology.

Scale 8 (Sc). The schizophrenic scale is designed to measure bizarre thoughts and reactions associated with schizophrenia. The MMPI notebook states, "HIGH Scale 8 scores suggest social withdrawal, unusual thought processes and nonconformity, *although not necessarily a schizophrenic condition.* LOW Scale 8 scores suggest a conventional, controlled, and somewhat compliant person likely to be seen by others as friendly and adaptable.[10]

Scale 9 (Ma). The hypomania scale measures the level of emotional excitement present in the individual. High scores indicate a high energy level (restlessness), while low scores indicate a low energy or activity level. Although Armstrong's scale 9 score is unusually high, the computer printed positive (as opposed to pathological) statements about his personality:

> He is an energetic enthusiastic person with broad interests and a tendency to become involved in a variety of activities. He is restless, enjoys change, and has little tolerance for monotony. He makes up his mind fast, changes it frequently, generally maintains a high level of activity, sometimes to the point of exhaustion.

Scale 10 (Si). The social introversion scale is designed to measure social participation. High scores suggest that the individual is not socially active and may feel socially inadequate. Low scores suggest an easy-going, socially acceptable personality.

Other MMPI scales are used upon occasion, and there are also various ways of reading the scales in conjunction with one another. The following is an excerpt from the MMPI notebook describing one form of profile analysis:

> The profile is frequently divided in terms of a neurotic side (left) and a psychotic side (right). Although this division is an oversimplification, it does have some utility as a rule of thumb for the visual inspection of profiles. By convention, scales 1, 2, and 3 are referred to as the "*neurotic triad*," and scales 6, 7, 8, and 9 as the "*psychotic tetrad*." When the neurotic triad is, on the average, higher than the psychotic tetrad, the profile is said to be negatively sloped (sloping downward), and in the reverse circumstance it is said to be positively sloped. Approximately equal elevation is referred to as a zero slope.
>
> It should be emphasized that the slope alone should not be used to derive a diagnosis, since much more sophisticated methods exist to make the differentiation. These latter techniques are included in the computer interpretation. The slope is introduced here to make MMPI profiles more meaningful. Often, a glance at a profile slope will help elucidate nuances of the narrative report. Positive slope generally signifies emotional disorders in which the person has poor reality contact, disorientation and confusion, and has difficulty maintaining control over his behavior and feelings. Negative slope, by contrast, generally indicates more acute emotional upsets characterized by anxiety, poor morale, and physical symptoms, but with better reality contact.[11]

Using the MMPI

Prosecutors can use the MMPI to their advantage. The case of Elizabeth Nicholas, indicted for the double murder of her parents, is a good example. Nicholas confessed to her psychiatrists and promptly filed notice of a mental disease. She had been institutionalized in various parts of the country intermittently since 1967. Over ten psychiatrists were willing to testify that she was insane, a paranoid schizophrenic. None was willing to say that she was not mentally deranged. Yet the results of an MMPI taken five months before the murder (and this could be very significant) showed her to be only depressed and socially inactive. (See figure 6-2.) Her profile shows that her paranoid, psychasthenic, and schizophrenic scores were all very normal. Since the neurotic triad is higher than the psychotic tetrad, Elizabeth Nicholas's profile is said to be negatively sloped, and negative slopes tend to suggest a much better reality contact than do positive slopes. This can be a key device for showing that the defendant could substantially conform her conduct to the requirements of law since the positive slope would indicate that she could not.

If a defendant appears normal on the MMPI profile and this fact is presented into evidence, the prosecutor can enlarge the profile into an exhibit and use it during argument. Since psychiatry is not exact and the MMPI profile appears scientifically sound, this approach can be persuasive, as the aggravated-murder trial of Rex Larsen shows. Larsen had executed a

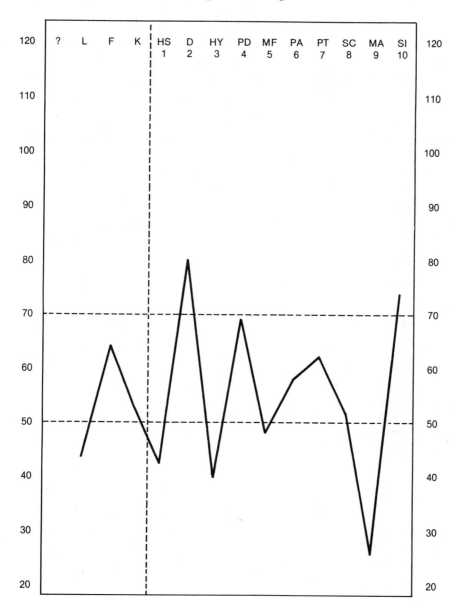

Figure 6-2. Elizabeth Nicholas: MMPI Profile

cab driver presumably because he wanted to assault sexually the cab driver's girlfriend, who was riding in the cab at the time. The defendant's mental defense was based partially on the testimony of a psychologist who had administered the Rorschach test and the Thematic Apperception Test to the defendant and concluded that defendant was a paranoid schizophrenic. The psychologist ignored the results of an MMPI given to the defendant a year earlier while the defendant was incarcerated. (The Oregon State Penitentiary routinely administers the MMPI to willing prisoners soon after admission.) Not surprisingly, the defendant's MMPI showed only an elevated social deviant scale. In addition to impeaching the other psychological tests, the MMPI provided an effective way to show the jury the defendant's ability to appear normal, at least in a prison situation where it was in his interest not to appear to be a paranoid schizophrenic. If the prosecutor can show that the defendant is capable of manipulating the psychological tests to his own benefit, the entire mental defense can be impeached. Even if he cannot show directly that the defense expert has been fooled into finding the defendant not responsible, he can at least accomplish this indirectly by proper use of the defendant's manipulation of the psychological tests. The psychiatrist for the prosecution probably will be able to support this thesis in his testimony.

Projective Tests

The MMPI, an objective compendium, represents the most widely used of the psychological tests. Projective tests, however, are also used quite frequently in criminal trials. They consist of relatively unstructured materials, which the patient is asked to organize and/or interpret. These tests are not designed to measure specific abilities but are intended to reveal the psychodynamic structure of an individual's personality. Unlike the automated MMPI, the test-giver's technique plays a vital role in the scoring of the projectives. Thus the test is open to attack on the basis of its subjectivity, and since the psychologist used his own cognitive powers to analyze the defendant's responses to the test, he will be forced to defend his results to a much greater degree than he would the results of the computerized MMPI. Since the projectives appear less scientific than the objective tests, they are easily criticized in court. One element of this criticism is in the description itself. The modern trend among psychologists is to call the projectives *techniques* rather than *tests*. Jurors should be made aware of this difference because *technique* sounds less credible than *test*. The two projective tests used most frequently in the courtroom are the Rorschach inkblot technique and the thematic apperception test (TAT).

Rorschach Inkblot Technique

The Rorschach consists of a series of cards on which various-shaped inkblots are printed. The subject is shown the cards one at a time and asked, "What might this be? What does this look like?" The responses are written down and the reaction time recorded by the psychologist. Some pictures are black and white, and others have colored inkblots. The psychologist who administers the Rorschach must give the patient the card, time the response, write down the response, and observe and write down his observations, all at the same time. Thus both his technique and the accuracy of his report may be questioned.

When the psychologist submits his findings, he will be open to legitimate abuse by the hostile attorney. The Rorschach is the easiest projective to ridicule. The prosecutor should have a set of Rorschach cards nearby. He should begin by asking the psychologist to be more specific about his analysis. He might be asked from which particular cards he elicited this response. Then he should be shown the cards and asked to explain which symbols meant what to the defendant. An adroit prosecutor can have the jury laughing at the inkblots. A word of caution is in order, however; the prosecutor should not ridicule the test by appealing to ignorance. Prosecutors have been criticized by the federal courts for ridiculing the Rorschach.[12] Ridicule is not necessary, because intelligent criticism of the Rorschach can be much more effective.

James McConnell has made some intriguing comments on the Rorschach test. He notes that when Hermann Rorschach first devised his famous test in the 1920s, it won almost immediate approval from the medical profession. The test is based on the assumption that an observer who is presented with an unstructured situation will tend to fill in the gaps with his own personality traits. McConnell criticizes the Rorschach test by stating that a person who takes the Rorschach test usually describes in an ambiguous manner what he has seen and how he interprets it. The problem is that the bias of the one administering and scoring the test becomes most important. As McConnell says, "In fact, . . . experiments have shown pretty clearly that the Rorschach test usually tells you a great deal more about the person who scored or interpreted the test than about the patient who took the test in the first place."[13]

Anastasi also criticizes the Rorschach test:

Nor can any encouragement be found in empirical studies of Rorschach validity. Despite a bibliography of over 2,000 publications on the Rorschach, the vast majority of interpretive relationships that form the basis of Rorschach scoring have never been empirically validated. The number of published studies that have failed to demonstrate a significant relation between Rorschach scores, combinations of scores, or global evaluations and relevant criteria, is truly impressive. The Rorschach was found to have little or no predictive or concurrent validity when checked against such criteria as psychiatric diagnosis, response to psychotherapy, various determinations of personality or intellectual traits in normal persons, success or failure in a wide variety of occupations in which personality qualities play an important part, and presence of various conflicts, fears, attitudes, or fantasies independently identified in patients. Those studies that appear to provide positive results have been shown to contain serious methodological defects.[14]

A prosecutor who employs an intelligent approach can make to the jury believe that a Rorschach is a lot of nonsense, and, by analogy, psychological testimony can be severely discredited. A well-planned cross-examination of the Rorschach technique can be severely damaging to the defense.

Thematic Apperception Test

TAT, a product of the Harvard Psychological Clinic, was introduced in 1935 by its coauthors, Morgan and Murray. It consists of a series of pictures showing people in a variety of contexts depicting ambiguous situations. The subject is given these instructions:

> This is a test of imagination, one form of intelligence. I am going to show you some pictures, one at a time; and your task will be to make up as dramatic a story as you can for each. Tell what has led up to the event shown in the picture, describe what is happening at the moment, what the characters are feeling and thinking; and then give the outcome. Speak your thoughts as they come to your mind. Do you understand? Since you have fifty minutes for ten pictures, you can devote about five minutes to each story. Here is the first picture.[15]

The subject is classified by the way he analyzes each picture.

One of the pictures can be described in this way (copyright problems prohibit a reproduction): in the foreground is a young girl holding books. In the background appears to be a farm. A man not wearing a shirt is working in the fields. His back faces the viewer. At the right-hand side of the picture, a woman stands looking at the man. She appears to be pregnant.

When a group of us from the Lane County District Attorney's Office went to take this test and speak with a psychologist frequently used as a witness (for both defense and prosecution) in criminal trials, he remarked that a description such as the one given would be interpreted as defensive. In other words, the subject would be holding back from showing his personality by refusing to elaborate. He indicated that a more appropriate response would be that the girl with the books in the foreground looks as if she is contemplating something. He then indicated that a psychotic response could be determined when a subject imputed thoughts to the girl. In other words, if a subject did not recognize that the girl was thinking about something, he is defensive; if he realizes that the girl is thinking about something but does not try to explain what she is thinking, then that is appropriate, since, according to this psychologist, there is no way anyone could actually know what the girl is thinking. This interpretation seemed inconsistent since the instructions say that "your task is to make up as dramatic a story as you can" and that "this is a test of imagination." We then asked if a person with a background in classical art would not impute thoughts to the subject. The psychologist indicated that this was one of the problems with the test and added that from a normal artistic person the response, although inclusive of imputing thoughts to the characters in the pictures, would be much more integrated than a psychotic response. This, of course, makes some sense, but the TAT is basically indefensible for much the same reasons as the Rorschach. Anastasi concludes:

> It is apparent that the TAT can provide rich material for personality research or for qualitative interpretation by an experienced clinician. But attempts to use it as an objective test in its present form could yield very misleading results. Also relevant is the finding that, like the Rorschach, the TAT has proved susceptible to examiner and situational variables. The interpersonal relation of examiner and subject influences TAT responses, as it influences the results of any interviewing technique.[16]

Conclusion

On the witness stand it is not uncommon for the psychologist to be stage-frightened, paranoid, and generally defensive. MacDonald states:

> In any professional activity there are instances of incompetence or poor judgment. Even otherwise well-qualified individuals may, under stress, lapse into incompetent performance. Under pressure of cross-examination a psychologist may be prone to errors which would seldom, if ever, occur under less stressful circumstances. The example below occurred after the psychologist slipped into a situation of interpretation in isolation.

> Q. You can tell from responses to Rorschach cards what his personality is like?
> A. From a global picture.
> Q. What response did he give to Card 4?
> A. He saw a frog.
> Q. And what significance do you attach to this answer, Doctor?
> A. This is not the response normal people give. People often see two boots.

Here the psychologist does not merely give an inadequate answer, but conveys the idea that (a) there is one and only one normal response to the card in question, (b) a frog response is prima facie evidence of abnormality, and (c) he functions in contradiction to his earlier claim that he evaluates personality from a global picture.[17]

A prosecutor should use the results of psychological testing carefully when the results indicate a lack of pathology. If the tests do show pathology or suggest a valid mental defense, he can do a little research and acquire the latest findings or studies on the test in question. Then he can help slide both the psychiatrist and the psychologist into relying heavily on the test results (it is likely that they will anyway) by pretending to be ignorant about all psychological tests. If the psychologist senses that the prosecutor understands little of the testing procedures, he will rest assured that his techniques will not be subject to attack. Once the trap is set, the prosecutor can use his knowledge to pick apart the witness's testimony.

Notes

1. Anne Anastasi, *Psychological Testing* (New York: Macmillan, 1977).

2. Philip Harrimon, *Handbook of Psychological Terms* (Totowa, N.J.: Littlefield, Adams and Co., 1965). The definitions of the terms used in the text are taken from this dictionary. Reprinted with permission.

3. Roche Psychiatric Service Institute, *The MMPI Test Booklet* (Nutley, N.J.: Roche Psychiatric Service Institute, 1970), p. 1.

4. Raymond Fowler, *The Clinical Use of the Automated MMPI* (Nutley, N.J.: Roche Psychiatric Service Institute, 1976), p. 15. Reprinted with permission.

5. *State* v. *Robert Armstrong*, 38 Or. App. 219, 589 P.2d 1174 (1979).

6. Ibid.

7. Fowler, *Clinical Use*, p. 3.

8. Ibid.

9. Harrimon, *Handbook*.

10. Fowler, *Clinical Use*, p. 4.

11. Ibid., pp. 11-12.

12. *U.S.* v. *Brawner*, 471 F.2d 969 (D.C. Cir., 1972). "It is unfortunate that the prosecutor's summation incorporated, as an approach to the projective tests: 'After all, they are just blots of ink.' The prosecutor, who speaks in court in behalf of the public interest, has a responsibility to refrain from know-nothing appeals to ignorance. The prosecutor is not free to offer his own opinions and attitudes on matters of expert knowledge, even in camouflaged form."

13. James McDonnell, "Doctors Are People Too," *Michigan State Bar Journal* 47 (October 1968).

14. Anastasi, *Psychological Testing*, p. 499.

15. H. Murray, *Thematic Apperception Test* (Cambridge: Harvard University Press, 1943):3.

16. Anastasi, *Psychological Testing*, p. 576.

17. John MacDonald, *Psychiatry and the Criminal* (Springfield, Ill.: Charles C. Thomas, 1976), p. 175.

7 Impeaching the Expert

Frequently the crux of an accused's defense where lack of responsibility has been raised lies in the testimony of an expert witness. In cases of this sort the prosecutor is in an excellent position because psychiatrists, by the very nature of their profession, are impeachable. The problem comes when the material facts of the crime are so unusual that lay witnesses establish the defendant's abnormality. In those cases, the defense psychiatrist corroborates rather than establishes the defendant's insanity. Of course, there is a big gap between psychiatric abnormalities and legal insanity, and making these distinctions evident to the jury is the prosecutor's primary goal.

Cases in which the facts themselves establish potential insanity and those in which the psychiatrist alone tries to establish legal insanity are quite different. The former are the more troubling; the latter are somewhat easier to handle. With respect to the type of cases in which the psychiatrist principally establishes the defense, the bullet method is preferable. In these situations (called *bullet cases*), every avenue of attack on a psychiatrist is relevant, and most methods should be effective. In an attack on his diagnosis by way of the facts, the diagnosis should be impeachable. By attacking the field of psychiatry, the diagnosis, of course, becomes less credible.

The first questions the prosecutor should ask the expert on cross-examination should be foundation questions concerning the lack of scientific proof involved in the art of psychiatry. An excellent set of cross-examination questions designed to impeach the whole field of psychiatry can be found in *Coping with Psychiatric and Psychological Testimony*.[1]

The cross-examination of the defense expert in *State* v. *Donald Simmons* provides a good example of this strategy:

Q. Doctor, isn't it true that psychiatry consists mostly of a number of theories about human behavior, none of which you can scientifically prove?

A. That's true.

Q. And isn't it true that there is a substantial body of scientific and professional literature to the effect that psychiatric diagnoses are not very reliable and not very accurate?

A. There probably is a substantial amount, yes. There's lots of controversy in the field.

Q. Hasn't research shown that psychiatrists tend to diagnose schizophrenia where it does not exist?

A. There have been cases of people that have been diagnosed as having schizophrenic illnesses by psychiatrists that have not had it.[2]

In this fashion, the expert is immediately put on the defensive because he is being forced to defend an essentially defenseless position. This approach will usually give the prosecutor another subtle psychological edge because the expert will be uncertain about how much his questioner knows about the field.[3]

It is crucial for the prosecutor to take extensive notes during the direct examination of the defense expert. Frequently the direct testimony itself will point out the weaknesses of the expert's opinion. In *State* v. *Ricky Russell*, the defendant was accused of grabbing a woman's breasts in a downtown area of city-center mall.[4] The position espoused by the defense psychiatrist was that Russell believed that there was a conspiracy afoot by all of the big-breasted women in the world to lure Russell into touching them, at which point they would scream rape. The defendant had taken the stand and indicated that he had touched the victim's necklace to see what would happen but had not touched her breast. The defense psychiatrist testified that Russell could not conform his conduct to the requirements of law and could not appreciate the criminality of his actions. It became apparent that the defense psychiatrist had not asked the defendant many questions bearing on the crime itself. Careful probing during cross-examination revealed the following:

Q. You indicated that the defendant recognized that it would be unlawful to touch a woman's breast, but he didn't perceive what he did as unlawful. Is that correct?
A. Well, he said that he didn't really try to touch her breast, he knew that that would be unlawful, that he would not do that unless it was in private and with the other person's consent.
Q. And did you then ask him if he knew it was unlawful to go up and touch a woman's necklace?
A. No, I did not inquire about that.
Q. Wouldn't that have helped you to determine whether he could appreciate the criminality of his act?
A. No, I don't believe that had any bearing on my conclusion.
Q. Why not?
A. Because he's not being tried on charges of touching somebody's necklace.
Q. But, doctor, he's charged with touching a woman's breast, and he perceives himself touching her necklace. And even though there is a difference in perception, if he knew that he shouldn't have touched her necklace doesn't that act of going towards her and touching some part of her body or an ornament that she was wearing show an unwarranted intrusion upon the woman?
A. I appreciate the thrust of your question, and I think that it would be so insignificant in the light of the other data that I have that I couldn't weight it heavily.

Q. Let's go into that data. What did you base your opinion on?
A. Well, I based my opinion on my observations of him, the thoughts that he reported, everything he manifested, the feelings that he seemed to be going through or not going through. It's an observation and examination of an intangible concept, a person's mind.
Q. Did you inquire into his sexual background?
A. I inquired into his legal background, I did not specifically elicit what I would call his sexual history.

The fact that the defense psychiatrist had not elicited a sexual history from the defendant in a sex case surely destroyed his credibility with the jury. It became a major factor in the trial and was effectively exploited during closing argument.

An effective test is to ask the expert if he has read a study conducted by Dr. David Rosenhan, "On Being Sane in Insane Places."[5] The study shows that psychiatrists and psychiatric personnel are willing and able to diagnose schizophrenia where it simply does not exist. Generally a mere description of the study will influence the jury.

In a recent case the following exchange occurred during cross-examination of the defense psychiatrist:

Q. Isn't it true that quite often schizophrenia is diagnosed when it does not exist?
A. I would have no way of answering that question.
Q. Have you read the study of Dr. David Rosenhan of Stanford University entitled *"On Being Sane in Insane Places?"*
A. I'm not familiar with the particular author you're quoting.
Q. Well, this is a fairly well-known study in the field. If I might describe the study, I think you might recall it.
A. All right.
Q. The situation was the Dr. Rosenhan, a psychologist, took eight graduate students in psychology, and they tried to gain admittance in twelve different psychiatric wards. And the way they did it was they went up and spoke to the people in charge of admissions and all complained of the same thing, which was hearing voices. And they had all been examined and were normal people beforehand, but they just exhibited this one trait where they kept complaining of hearing weird voices. They were all immediately diagnosed schizophrenic and spent from three to fifty-two days in the hospitals before being released, and when they were all released, they were given the diagnoses, schizophrenia in remission. Are you aware of that study?
A. No, sir, I'm not aware of that study. But I could sure pick holes in it.
Q. I don't know if we should get into it if you haven't read the study.
A. All right.

This dialogue accomplished three purposes. First, the jury heard the summary of the study. Second, it pointed up a deficiency in the expert's background since he had not heard of the study. Third, in this case the doctor was ready to pick holes in something he had not read.

Often psychiatrists render an opinion as to the dangerousness of the defendant in their written reports to the defense attorney. Although the subject of dangerousness is inadmissible during the guilt phase of a trial, it may be admissible for impeachment purposes. If a psychiatrist (or psychologist) states that a subject will or will not be dangerous, there is a method of getting him to admit that he does not possess the powers of prediction.

In a recent case, *Tarasoff* v. *Board of Regents of the University of California*, the California Supreme Court ruled that when a psychotherapist believes that a patient presents a serious danger to a third person, the psychotherapist has a duty to warn the third person of that danger.[6] The facts of the *Tarasoff* case were that a patient of a University of California psychotherapist killed a young woman, Tatania Tarasoff. Several months before the murder, the patient allegedly told his psychotherapist that he intended to kill Tarasoff. The psychotherapist had the campus police detain the patient briefly, but, upon the request of the psychotherapist's superior, no further action was taken, and the victim was never warned. The irony of the case is that the American Psychiatric Association filed an amicus curiae brief in the case urging the court not to impose the newly created duty because psychiatrists and psychologists do not have the ability to predict dangerousness. (See appendix D.) The brief states, "This newly established duty to warn imposes an impossible burden upon the practice of psychotherapy. It requires the psychotherapist to perform a function which study after study has shown he is ill equipped to undertake; namely, the prediction of his patients' potential dangerousness." Then it continues, "The newly imposed duty to warn is also inconsistent with the finding of scientific research that no special ability or expertise has yet been demonstrated in the prognosis of dangerousness. Instead, the few studies which have been done strongly suggest that psychiatrists are rather inaccurate predictors."[7] A psychiatrist who does predict dangerousness or lack thereof should be impeached with the official position of the American Psychiatric Association as revealed in the *Tarasoff* brief.

A technique that often provides excellent impeachment material is to ask the expert what sources of information the expert opinion is based upon. Whatever the answer is, the prosecutor can destroy the psychiatrist's opinion by attacking the foundation. If, for example, psychological test data provided him with useful information, the tests can be attacked to show that the information relayed was not reliable and thus was useless. If his opinion is based in part upon a former hospital report labeling the defendant as a schizophrenic, the labeling system employed by psychiatric personnel can be attacked. The most thorough way of attacking the foundation upon which an expert has based an opinion is to ask him to name the informational sources. Usually a psychiatrist will list a personal interview with the defendant, police reports in the case, contact with family members, and data from psychological testing. Then the prosecutor can make inquiry into each of these sources. For example, the personal interview with the defendant frequently occurs from thirty to sixty days after the crime date. Yet the psychiatrist is giving an opinion on the defendant's mental state at the time of the crime. This exercise in forensic hindsight should be made obvious to the jury. Frequently the psychiatrist will use psychological test data in support of his opinion, but these materials themselves can be used to destroy the effect of those data. The important technqiue to be utilized in that situation, however, is to get the psychiatrist to commit himself first before the prosecution destroys the worth of the psychological tests. For example:

Q. Doctor, what technical data did you use in arriving at your opinion?
A. I had the aid of several psychological tests that were given to the defendant.
Q. What tests?
A. The defendant took the Minnesota Multi-Phasic Personality Inventory, the Rorschach Inkblot Projective Test, the Make-a-Picture Projective Test, and the Thematic Apperception Test.
Q. And did these tests actually help you in arriving at your opinion? Or, did you rely on these tests in reaching your opinion?
A. Yes, to some extent.

The last answer is the typical response. It is very difficult to get the expert to commit himself entirely. At this point it is useful to ask the doctor to explain the tests (and their results) before asking him if he relied on them. He may be foolish enough to say that they were a big part of the reason he arrived at his particular opinion. If he does, the prosecutor will have laid a most ingenious trap because all of those tests are less reliable than a malfunctioning polygraph.

If the doctor has not relied on psychological data, one technique is to have the tests performed by the state's psychologist. If the tests tend to show psychopathology, the defense psychiatrist should be given copies of the tests. This will tend to bolster his opinion, and it may be possible to get him to commit himself to the tests in any case. If the tests contradict his opinion, they can still be used to impeach his opinion. The strategy should be to get him to say the tests are worthless. Then he should be asked to explain why they are so often used by psychotherapists. The following dialogue presents an example:

Q. Doctor, you've indicated that in your opinion the defendant is a paranoid schizophrenic?
A. Yes.
Q. Are you familiar with the Minnesota Multi-Phasic Personality Inventory?
A. Yes.

Q. What is it?
A. It is a series of 550 items to which a patient responds true or false. The results are tabulated and used to form a psychological profile.
Q. Isn't it true that the MMPI is the most widely used psychological test in the world?
A. Yes.
Q. And isn't it also true that the MMPI has both a paranoia scale and a schizophrenic scale?
A. That's correct.
Q. Then how do you explain the fact that according to the MMPI that the defendant took, both the paranoia scale and the schizophrenia scale show that he is normal and that there is no indiction that the defendant has a schizophrenic personality?

At this point the doctor will have to discredit the test, but the damage has already been done. In addition, the prosecutor can bring in a psychologist in rebuttal to say what a useful tool the MMPI is. Of course, if the defense counsel is aware of the test's shortcomings, it probably is not a good idea to put on a psychologist for the purpose of rebuttal.

After attacking the psychological data, the prosecutor should ask if the expert has read all of the police reports. These reports are very important because they are usually made at or near the time of the crime. In addition, it is useful to ask the doctor if he interviewed any eyewitnesses to the crime. If he replies that he has not, it will hurt his credibility. The prosecutor can then argue that the expert relied on a supposedly mentally diseased defendant (with an obvious bias), as opposed to objective and disinterested eyewitnesses, for an accounting of the crime.

In *State* v. *Ernest Banuelos*, the defendant was charged with armed robbery.[8] The defense was insanity. The defendant had gone into a variety store armed with a shotgun and demanded all of the money in the store. The cashier triggered an alarm. The defendant heard the alarm go off and ran out of the store without the money. When the police caught up with him, he told them that when he heard the alarm, he knew it was too risky to stay, so he left without the money. The defense psychiatrist submitted a report saying that the defendant could not appreciate the criminality of his conduct, nor could he conform his conduct to the requirements of law. However, on direct examination, he testified that the defendant could appreciate the criminality of his act but that he could not conform his conduct. By asking the expert what sources he relied upon, the prosecutor discovered that the defense attorney had provided the expert with only those police reports that tended to show unusual actions by the defendant. In a classic confrontation, the prosecutor was able to annihilate the defense and discredit the defense counsel simultaneously. Part of that cross-examination follows:

Q. How about the defendant's statement, "I walked in the store and could have blown them dudes away, but I didn't. I could have." Were you familiar with that?

A. I don't think that is in the reports that I have.
Q. Okay. If the defendant made that statement shortly after he was arrested, within a couple of hours. Would that be of some significance to you?
A. Certain amount of reality testing going on.
Q. And you would have some indication that he had the capacity to conform because he made a decision not to shoot?
A. Perhaps.
Q. At least, he realized that he could have, but he didn't do it?
A. For one reason or another.
Q. Did he indicate to you or were you aware that when he heard this alarm ringing, he believed it was just too risky to stay inside the store?
A. He didn't indicate to me he heard the alarm ring.
Q. Assume that he heard an alarm and he felt it was some kind of a burglar alarm or robbery alarm. Would the fact that he then appreciated that the police would be coming soon be of any significance in your opinion?
A. Again, certain evidence of reality testing.
Q. What does that mean?
A. That he could perceive what was happening accurately.
Q. And then, despite the fact that he knew that he went there to get money, and hearing this alarm, and appreciating this risk and leaving without the money, would that indicate the same thing?
A. Yes.
Q. Did he indicate to you that he backed away from the store, then ran to his van and told his companion, "Let's get out of here"?
A. Yes.
Q. Is that consistent with him appreciating that he had done something against the law?
A. I think he could appreciate the criminality, yes.
Q. Oh, you do think he could appreciate the criminality of the conduct?
A. That is what I said on direct.
Q. Okay. Well, have you done some rethinking of his condition since this report was written? [In the report, the expert had concluded that the defendant could not appreciate the criminality of his conduct.]
A. No.
Q. In the report, I read it to conclude that you believe the defendant had a defense of mental disease or defect on both grounds; that he couldn't appreciate the criminality of his conduct, nor could he conform? Am I reading that incorrectly?
A. Yes, you are. That is not what I responded on direct. I said I thought he undoubtedly appreciated the criminality of what was going on, but he really was in such a state that he couldn't really conform.
Q. If he could appreciate that he could get caught and then stopped short of committing the full act, isn't that extremely strong evidence that he could conform?
A. Not necessarily. All these discrepancies you are bringing up is the very reason I established the diagnosis I did. If he could have given me exactly the same history as he told the police and seemed to be clear and definite on it, it would have been different, but there was much confusion in his thinking, and that is what concerned me.
Q. Well, that is not very confusing, is it, the fact that he actually did, as he told the police, hear the alarm and leave the store before getting the money because he was afraid to get caught?

A. That is not what he told me.

Q. Assume that is what he told the police. If that is the case, if that is what he was really thinking at the time of the robbery, then he could, in fact, wouldn't you agree, conform his conduct. and did conform it to the extent that he terminated it—

A. Terminated his behavior—

Q. —so he could get away?

A. —in order to avoid violating a law, getting shot, getting apprehended, or something, yes.

Q. And if that is what he was really thinking, would your opinion still be the same as it is?

A. If that is what he was really thinking, but this is certainly contrary to what he told me.

Q. I guess I didn't get it answered. If that is what he was really thinking—that is, "I had better get out of here. I hear the alarm. The police are coming. I will have to leave the money," if that is what he was thinking, would your opinion be different?

A. If that is what he was thinking, then I would say he was able to conform his conduct.

Since the prior evidence had established the facts set forth in these questions, the defense psychiatrist became the prosecutor's star witness.

Another approach is to attack the system of terminology classification used by psychiatrists. One possible approach follows:

Q. Doctor, do you use the American Psychiatric Association's *Diagnostic and Statistical Manual of Mental Disorder* as a classification system?

A. Yes.

Q. Do you rely on the definitions set forth in the manual?

A. Yes.

Q. Isn't there a lot of controversy in the field concerning the reliability of the manual?

A. Yes.

Q. Now isn't it true that mental diseases, as defined by the manual, are established by vote and not through scientific experiments?

A. Yes.

Q. For example, isn't it true that several years ago the APA took a vote and decided that homosexuality was not a mental disease?

A. Yes.

Q. But isn't it also true that out of 9,644 psychiatrists who voted almost 4,000 voted to make homosexuality a mental disease?

A. I don't remember the figures.

Q. Isn't it *possible*, doctor, that next year the APA could vote to reclassify schizophrenia so as not to make it a mental disease?

A. Yes.

Q. And isn't it true that the foreword to the manual states, referring to schizophrenia, that the APA "could not establish agreement about what the disorder is, it could only agree on what to call it?"

A. I don't know.

If the expert takes issue with any questions regarding the APA manual, Ziskin states that other areas that complicate the proper classification of mental illness include terminology:

> Terms such as "schizophrenia," "paranoid," "sociopath," "personality disorder," make frequent appearances in courtrooms. The impression is often given that these represent well-defined disease entities or syndromes or behavioral or emotional patterns. The fact is that they are not well defined nor well established, nor accepted, even though they may be in widespread use. The official terminology is that of the American Psychiatric Association's Diagnostic and Statistical Manual of Mental Disorders. The terms and definitions therein have not been arrived at on the basis of research and experimentation, but rather on the *astonishingly unscientific procedure of majority vote*. . . . The real significance of the action is its demonstration of the lack of objective criteria for mental illness upon which most professionals could agree and the dependence of a finding of mental illness on the subjective values and attitudes of psychiatrists. While on this basis one might argue that this terminology and classification system has been accepted, it could hardly be said that it has been accepted by a *scientific* community, in view of the procedures by which it has been adopted. *Scientists* proceed by research, not by vote.[9]

Suggestions for avenues of impeachment could run on forever. It is important to confront the expert with the facts of the case. All other suggestions by necessity must attack the general foundation of the doctor's expertise. A good area to close with is the value of his opinion:

Q. Doctor, isn't it true that psychiatrists often differ in their diagnoses of the same patient?
A. Yes.
Q. And your diagnosis is basically your opinion, isn't that correct?
A. Based on my training and experience, yes.
Q. Do you do any follow-up evaluations of your previous diagnoses?
A. No.
Q. Then you have no scientific proof that your opinion is any more reliable than a psychiatrist with a different opinion?
A. No, I don't.

Few psychiatrists will change their opinion or concede even minor points on the witness stand. All, however, must admit to the lack of scientific method involved in their work. A prosecutor can sometimes make them look foolish, and can always dent their professional armor. A prosecutor who will be calling a psychiatrist for the state must proceed with caution, however, for in destroying the field of psychiatry, he may invariably destroy his own expert's credibility. Therefore, the materials presented here are to be used selectively to obtain the right formula for a particular case. For example, the defense psychiatrist may claim that the defendant is a paranoid schizophrenic who decompensated into an active psychosis at the time of the crime and therefore was unable to conform his conduct to the requirements of law. The prosecution may have some reliable data that indicate goal-directed behavior by the defendant before and after the crime. He also plans to use a psychiatrist who will say that the defendant is a sociopath. Under these circumstances the prosecutor could attack psychiatry, its labeling of mental disease, its inability to determine accurately after the fact whether a particular defendant was actively psychotic during the crime, and the speculative nature of the ultimate conclusion that the defendant could not conform. The state's psychiatrist should not be damaged by this attack because he would be relying heavily on the defendant's antisocial background and the facts of the crime to reach his opinion. In other words, he will be making common-sense conclusions. The jurors will be able to relate to him, while they may not to the defense psychiatrist, who will be necessarily relying upon psychiatric hypothesis, probably based mainly on what the defendant had told him. This was just what happened in *State* v. *Johnny Bruno*.[10] In this well-publicized case, the defendant and two others were charged with killing and dismembering the defendant's wife, Pam Bruno. The defendant raised a mental defense related to intoxication. His defense expert testified that he believed the defendant's story that he could not remember the crime and that he really loved his wife. Also, under "truth serum," defendant had told the doctor he was at a friend's house the night the crime was committed. Based upon this, the doctor said that the defendant could not have had the mental capacity to commit a crime. His opinion seemed ridiculous in light of the defendant's multiple confessions to police (including a videotaped reenactment of the crime) and testimony from acquaintances that the defendant hated his wife and that he was not at the friend's house on the night in question.

Notes

1. J. Ziskin, *Coping with Psychiatric and Psychological Testimony* (Beverly Hills: Law and Psychology Press, 1970).

2. *State* v. *Donald Simmons*, Lane County (Oregon) District Court No. B41-402 (1977).

3. James McDonnell, "Doctors Are People Too," *Michigan State Bar Journal* 47 (October 1968):12-25.

4. *State* v. *Ricky Russell*, Lane County (Oregon) District Court No. 78-170.

5. D. Rosenhan, "On Being Sane in Insane Places," *Science* 179 (1973):250-258.

6. *Tarasoff* v. *Board of Regents of the University of California*, 17 Cal. 3d 425 (1975).

7. Quoted in A. Dershowitz, "The Law of Dangerousness," *Journal of Legal Education* 23 (1970):24-53.

8. *State* v. *Ernest Banuelos*, Lane County (Oregon) Circuit Court No. 76-274.

9. Ziskin, *Coping*, p. 104.

10. *State* v. *Johnny Bruno*, Lane County (Oregon) Circuit Court No. 79-1761.

8 Cross-Examining the Defendant

Very often the defendant in a mental case will not testify. Generally a sympathetic psychiatrist can present a defendant's story better than the defendant himself can. Also the defendant might be caught in lies, which will help destroy much of the credibility of his examining psychiatrist, who will necessarily rely upon the defendant's statements. In criminal cases, generally a defendant might not testify because his prior record will be used to impeach him. In a mental case, his record will come out through psychiatrists, but it will be for a different purpose. The clever defense psychiatrist may even use the defendant's many convictions to his advantage. If a defendant takes the stand, he takes the chance of sounding sane. In addition, the craziest defendants might insist that they are sane, and it is a calculated risk for a defense attorney to put his client on the stand. Many defendants simply do not want to be labeled insane and be institutionalized. Therefore, it is likely that prosecutors will have few opportunities to cross-examine a defendant in a mental-defense trial.

Should the opportunity arise, the prosecution should begin by trying to establish a logical dialogue with the defendant. Trivialities can be important because they can help to establish that the defendent performed in a logically coherent manner on the witness stand. This can later be used in argument to prove the defendant's sanity. If the defendant does not make sense during questioning, the prosecutor should get sarcastic and out of hand himself in order to make it seem like a big game that both are playing. If the defendant has confessed, the statement should be gone over in detail. This provides an opportunity to emphasize the areas where the defendant's statements or acts indicate rational, goal-oriented behavior. The prosecutor should make an extensive list of all such rational statements or acts, which can be used for cross-examination of the defendant and defense experts, as well as for his own experts and in final argument.

If possible, the prosecutor should establish any of the defendant's attempts at making himself look mentally unstable. If it can be shown that he was faking just one time, the entire defense can be discredited.

The prosecutor should beware of the defendant who does take the stand in an insanity trial. Obviously his attorney thinks that the defendant will appear unbalanced. Thus the prosecutor must select his questions carefully so as not to set the defendant off on a wild tangent. The case of *State* v. *William Carney*, where the defendant was charged with public indecency, provides a good example.[1] Carney fired his first attorney because the attorney had filed notice of intent to rely on a mental defense. The defendant was sure that he was not crazy. His second attorney, with the defendant's permission, filed notice of intent to rely on partial responsibility.[2]

The defendant waived jury, and the state called two female witnesses, who testified that the defendant had come into a church where they worked, pulled out his penis, and started massaging it. The defendant took the stand and admitted that what the women had said was basically true, with one major exception. He testified that he and the women had reached an agreement whereby he would expose himself, and they would allow him to do so. When asked why they had agreed, the defendant said that a rumor had been circulating that he did not have a penis and that he had to prove to them that he had one. Although it was subsequently proved that no such conversation had taken place, the damage was done. The doctrine of partial responsibility could have acquitted him because the state's burden was to prove that he had the intent to arouse himself sexually during the incident.

Based on the defendant's delusional thinking, it appeared as if he could not form the intent of arousing himself, since he was only trying to prove that he in fact had a penis. On cross-examination, the prosecutor took several chances, which paid off. The defendant had been massaging his penis, and that did not seem consistent with his plan. The theory was to point this inconsistency out to him and see how he handled it. If he lied, his story could be discredited as less than a delusion. The following segment of the cross-examination shows that there were no inconsistencies in his tale:

Q. You say that you're a normal male physically, is that correct?
A. Yeah, well, there was a rumor going around that I wasn't.
Q. But you are, right?
A. Yeah.
Q. You're subject to the same desires that other males are subject to, would you agree?
A. Sure, right, correct.
Q. There's nothing different about you in that respect.
A. No.
Q. Why were you massaging your penis?
A. Cause I told you that the. . .they. . .the reason for that is because there was a rumor going around that I did not have a penis.
Q. Okay.
A. And it—the best way to break up a rumor like that is to show it to somebody. And I don't—I been wanting to go to a doctor.
Q. Okay, but you could have showed it to them without massaging it, isn't that correct?
A. Uh, yeah, but the—then they could still say you're a concubine, this is—if it's a little hard, it's uh, see . . .
Q. Oh, so you wanted to erect yourself . . .
A. That's right
Q. . . . and to show them, is that correct?
A. That's correct, I wanted an erection. The reason for that is cause concubines do have their penis. But it doesn't get hard.

Q. So that in essence you did want to arouse yourself sexually to show them that you have a penis.

A. That's correct. That was my sole intent. I'd do it all again just to disprove these vicious rumors that get started.

The defendant's testimony on cross-examination proved that he could form the intent to commit the crime because the intent to arouse himself was part of his plan. He was responsible.

The art of cross-examining a zany defendant may not always be successful. The important point to remember is to pick a narrow objective and to stick with it. A defendant with mental problems should not be provided chance to prove his lack of capacity to their trier of fact.

The defendant should be questioned about the details of the crime as much as possible. He may admit facts that will help the state's case. Even if he does not, he will probably be caught lying. Either way, the state benefits. A successful prosecutor will delve into certain areas of his background and avoid others. For example, if the defendant has been convicted previously, the fact of conviction should be established. Then he can be asked if he raised a mental defense. If he answers affirmatively, all will know that the defense was not successful. If he says "no," he can be asked why (although this is a risky question), or the prosecutor can simply wait to comment in argument that if the defendant was really not criminally responsible, one would have expected him to raise the defense to the earlier charge(s).

When the defendant does not testify and his statements are made only second-hand by his psychiatrist who has relied on their accuracy in formulating his opinion, the state's closing argument should expose the weakness of such evidence. This is a somewhat risky maneuver and must be dealt with carefully to avoid the claim that the state is improperly commenting on the defendant's failure to testify; however, an argument such as the following should be permissible:

> Dr. X has said his opinion is predicated upon his believing the defendant's statements about what was going through the defendant's mind at the time of the crime. Of course, if defendant's statements aren't reliable, then the doctor's opinion isn't either. Ask yourselves the question; Knowing what I know about the defendant's background, would I be willing to convict someone else based upon the defendant's second-hand statements to his psychiatrist if the defendant was the only witness to the crime? The answer should be *NO*!

Notes

1. *State* v. *William Carney*, Lane County (Oregon) District Court No. 77-857.

2. ORS 161.300 says, "Evidence that the actor suffered from a mental disease or defect is admissible whenever it is relevant to the issue of whether he did or did not have the intent which is an element of the crime." Originally ORS 161.300 was an affirmative defense, and the defendant had the burden of proof. However, the recent case of *State* v. *Stockett*, 278 Or. 637, 565 P.2d 739 (1977), held ORS 161.300 to be unconstitutional insofar as it placed the burden of proof with regard to intent on the defendant, contrary to *Mullaney* v. *Wilbur* 44 L.E.d2d 508 (1975). Therefore, at the time of *State* v. *William Carney*, the state had the burden of disproving the mental defense of partial responsibility beyond a reasonable doubt.

Obtaining, Preparing, and Examining the State's Expert

This phase is the most delicate part of a mental-defense trial, for in attacking the psychiatric profession the prosecutor has left a difficult path for his own expert to traverse. Thus he must decide what testimony he wishes to elicit from his expert so as to avoid issues that may hurt his own credibility with the jury.

Basically, there are two kinds of experts that the prosecutor should look for, based on a given strategy. If he wishes to destroy the credibility of psychiatry during a criminal trial, he should seek an antiexpert expert like Jay Ziskin.[1] Ziskin will testify to the lack of reliability of psychiatric evidence. Few other experts will do the same, however, because it will permanently destroy their future effectiveness in the courtroom when testifying as a straight expert. The antiexpert expert would, of course, go hand in hand with the materials in this book, but most of the time the state probably will be pursuing the one-on-one method. Whichever approach it takes, the state needs the very best expert it can obtain.

The key to employing a psychiatrist successfully for the state is in the preparation of the case. The expert's eventual testimony in most cases will be a free-flowing affair based on a common strategy devised by the expert and state's attorney. First they must analyze all of the information available about the defendant and the crime. They must explore all possible defenses and potential theories for lack of responsibility.

The state's attorney should try to predict what theory he would use based on the available evidence in the case if he were the defense attorney. Then he should imagine what he would do to counter the defense theory. Only when he believes that he can, can he select the appropriate expert. This analysis should be done as close to the time of the incident as possible since it is the defendant's mental state at the time of the crime that is at issue.

Not much time should elapse before he schedules a psychiatric examination for the defendant with his own expert. The prosecutor should discuss his theories with the psychiatrist before the interview takes place. The psychiatrist will then be in a position to elicit information from the defendant that will either help the theory or cause the prosecutor to look for another. If the defendant permits questioning about the crime, the psychiatrist should ask questions to help uncover more evidence of what took place. This is particularly important in homicide cases, since there may be no eyewitnesses. Whatever the defendant says can help. He may provide more information or he may provide lies that the state can disprove and thereby discredit the whole mental defense. In any event the prosecuting attorney.should advocate his position to test the psychiatrist. If the doctor takes an opposite view, he can be used to test out the potential cross-examination of the defense expert.

The prosecutor should supply the expert with all the evidence available, including information that could be helpful to defense. It can be very damaging to have the defense attorney ask the state's expert a series of questions dealing with bizarre incidents in the defendant's history and have the expert acknowledge that he was unaware of them. He will most likely find a way to explain the damaging evidence in terms compatible with his opinion. This, of course, is the great weakness in psychiatry; almost anything can be explained by an alternate hypothesis.

Once the prosecutor is aware that a defendant intends to use a mental defense, it is wise to have the defendant observed by a state-employed psychologist or psychiatrist as soon as possible. In extraordinary cases, a psychiatrist should observe the defendant on the date of the crime. The nearer the examination to the crime, the more credible the expert's opinion will appear to be. If an expert is not available, consider videotaping the defendant. If the defendant is talking coherently about the crime, so much the better, but it will also be helpful to simply show him responding to orders or answering general questions at a book-in proceeding. This expert need not be the one who eventually examines him for trial purposes. It may be helpful to have the jail's psychologist write down his observations and turn them over to the examining psychiatrist. This procedure is helpful because conditions in county jails are usually terrible. Anybody, sane or insane, is going to have difficulty remaining mentally healthy in a county jail. Frequently prisoners have mental breakdowns after spending considerable time in county jails. Therefore it is important to note the defendant's composure when he first arrives in jail so that his mental state at a later time may be compared with his condition at or near the time of the crime.

There is another reason for finding a psychiatrist so early in a criminal case. Frequently by the time an expert makes an opinion, the crime is remote and somewhat unreal. The doctor sees the defendant in an actual situation, and human nature may tend to make the doctor sympathetic with the defendant's predicament. However, if the psychiatrist is actually aware of the victim and aware of concrete evidence of the crime, the sympathy factor may be balanced. Dr. Bernard L. Diamond confirms that the expert witness "does become an advocate. Because his testimony does in fact support one side of the legal battle, he, if he is at all human, must necessarily identify himself with his own opinion, and subjectively desire that 'his side' win."[2]

During the psychiatric examination, the defendant generally does not have to answer questions concerning the crime.[3] However, he must answer all other questions, or the defense may be stricken,[4] or the state may comment on the defendant's refusal to answer questions.[5] It is doubtful whether *Miranda* warnings are necessary, but it would be safer to have the expert administer these warnings to the defendant.[6] Since *Shepard* v. *Bowe*, it has been common practice in Oregon for the defendant to have his attorney present at the psychiatric examination; however, this is not a judicially promulgated rule of law and is subject to challenge. In *State ex rel. Jonhson* v. *Woodrich*, the Oregon Supreme Court reaffirmed *Shepard* v. *Bowe*, holding that the state cannot compel incriminating evidence from the defendant during a psychiatric examination. Given this ruling, it is doubtful that the defendant has a Sixth Amendment right to counsel at an examination that has already been limited to protect the defendant's consititutional rights.

The psychiatrist should be informed of the current status of the law before the examination so that he knows what questions he is trying to answer. After the examination has been conducted, the prosecutor should ask the psychiatrist for an oral opinion and discuss any new evidence that has been discovered subsequent to the examination. Then the expert should prepare a written report.

Since the report is a formality, it is best to delay its preparation until shortly before trial. Then the witness will be able to state that before he reached his final decision, he had most, if not all, of the information available. The report should be short because it will often provide the primary vehicle for cross-examination and impeachment. For example, reports should contain the following information:

1. Name of agency requesting examination;
2. Time, place and length of each examination;
3. Reason for examination;
4. Type of examination;
5. Information available to examiner;
6. Account of defendant's personal background;
7. Doctor's diagnosis;
8. Facts of case upon which doctor relies in forming diagnosis or opinion, including any other psychological or neurological tests;
9. Opinion as to each of the questions asked, answered, in the appropriate statutory language.[7]

After the report has been submitted, the prosecutor and his expert should discuss his testimony during the trial. Some experts prefer to be directed carefully by the prosecutor during their entire direct testimony, while others like to be able to proceed by soliloquy. This conference will aid in preparing the rebuttal phase of the case, and the expert will also be able to spot the weakness in the defense expert's opinion and be able to steer the prosecutor to the opposing expert's weak points. If the prosecutor is planning to impeach the defense psychiatrist with several psychiatric articles, the state's expert must read them thoroughly so he can explain the treatises to the jury. Rosenhan's "On Being Sane in Insane Places" is useful for the expert to read so that the jury can be made aware of the vulnerability of psychiatric diagnoses.[8]

When the psychiatrist takes the stand, the first step is to qualify him as an expert. He should review his education, pointing out his speciality, the length of his experience, any honors he has received, whether he is a member of the APA, whether he is certified, if he has any teaching experience, and whether he is licensed to practice his specialty in the jurisdiction. The next step is to ask him if he has testified in court before and if he has been qualified as an expert witness previously. The prosecution must never accept a stipulation of qualifications from the defense because those qualifications must be put in front of the jury. True, they are somewhat meaningless, but if an expert is being used, his credentials need to be set forth. If defense counsel has offered to stipulate to the expert's qualifications in the jury's presence, the prosecutor should always refuse politely but comment upon this in his closing argument.

After the expert has been presented as qualified to testify, he should be asked to state what materials he has reviewed with regard to the present inquiry. Then he should be asked for his opinion. His answers should be presented in the statutory language because that is the language that the judge will use to instruct the jury. One tactical approach is to keep the direct testimony short and to the point, leaving it to the defense counsel to open up any dangerous areas. If the expert is a good witness, he will embarrass an unsuspecting attorney. In *State* v. *Ernest Banuelos*, the state's expert was an exceedingly competent witness. His psychiatric report follows:

Pursuant to court order of the Circuit Court of the State of Oregon for Lane County, Mr. Banuelos was examined psychiatrically on June 28, 1976 at the County Court House in Eugene, Oregon. The examination lasted about two hours. Mr. Banuelos was clad in jail attire. He was soft spoken, courteous, had an air of fatigue or tiredness. When asked if he was sleepy or tired, he disclaimed that he was. His attention or attitude varied with the subject matter at hand.

I informed him that he was talking to me as an evaluator of his mental condition; that it was ordered by the court, and that it wasn't a treatment situation; that the information we discussed could be aired in court. He said he understood this. He was comfortable, showed no difficulty with movement, no physical discomfort.

This gentleman was born in Azusa, California, on September 21, 1952. This is an area about 25 to 30 miles east of Los Angeles. He was the second youngest of six children; all siblings being female. He's never been married. His parents are alive and well, and divorced. He didn't finish high school.

He received rather poor grades; denies being arrested as a juvenile; worked at a car-wash part-time while he was in high school, and about a year thereafter. He quit school because he was angry when they informed him he couldn't graduate by taking subjects as repeats. He was treated at Norwalk Metropolitan Hospital on a voluntary basis in about 1975, because he states he overdosed himself on Seconal or "Reds." States he was also treated in Camarillo State Hospital in California in about 1972; this again for depression. He denies having taken any medication when he left the hospital or having any recommended to him. He denies any knowledge of any diagnosis during his hospitalizations. He states he has had normal heterosexual relationships, denies any homosexuality. He *"can't imagine anything so important* that I *would go to work for it."* He supports himself by working very little and "bumming" most of the time. He thinks it's okay to borrow money from people and not pay them back. He attended church as he grew up, but he "learned nothing."

Mental Status Exam: He's oriented to time, place, and person. He tends to be a bit covert. He wants to seem confused and out of it; however, when you press him for answers he can give them in an intelligent manner. Tends to say "I don't know" quite often.

He interprets the proverb "Crying Over Spilt Milk", correctly; "Don't get upset over something you can't change". He refuses to try on more sophisticated proverbs. Word similarities are done acceptably. He has no trouble with Serial Sevens. Knowledge of current events reflects his lackadaisical and disinterested approach to life. He feels, on occasion, he's not been himself. He describes this as being lonely. He feels that occasionally he has thoughts to hurt other people. He sometimes thinks the Devil controls his thoughts, but this is said with a bit of a grin; a rather disinterested type of response. He can't describe any auditory hallucinations. He is "stoned" on drugs a great deal of the time, and when he's not on drugs, he can't remember ever losing control of his thoughts. He has no plans for the future. He answers it, "Whatever comes first," "I really don't care". He describes himself as being an impatient person, who's "bored easily". He disclaims any understanding of what laws are for. He doesn't agree with most laws, he states; and he states, *"If we break them, we go to jail"*. He claims he learned nothing by attending church, as mentioned above. Doesn't feel that other people have too many rights. He feels that if people have sufficient goods, it's okay to steal from them, and he states, "There's nothing in the world I want enough to go to work for". He has lived in foster homes some of his life. He was in a boys' home when he was about fourteen, started drinking about that time. He went to a foster home originally because his step-dad did not treat him right. He was first arrested at age eighteen. *When asked if he'd ever been "crazy" when not "tripped out on drugs"*, he answers, "No, not that I can remember."

He seems cognizant of the evening's activities leading up to the arrest. He remembers the fight between Dave and Don. He indicates that Klein didn't say much for or against holding up the store, and that Klein was more or less looking for friends as he "had nobody out there". He indicates they were *going to get money to pay Klein back for using his van,* as he had sort of played chauffeur for them for a while. He indicates that had there been a *Police Car or an authority* figure *on the premises, that he would have responded as, "I would have gone away"*.

Throughout the psychiatric evaluation he was very covert. He tended to wish to appear confused, as mentioned above; wished to appear to be less aware than he really is, less direct or contemplative than he actually is. I can detect no frank thought disorder in Mr. Banuelos.

Diagnostic Impression: Personality disorder, anti-social personality.

It is my professional opinion that Mr. Banuelos is now, and was on March 26 and March 27 of 1976, free of any mental disease or defect that would serve to exculpate him from his activities.[9]

The defense counsel seized upon the proverb "Don't cry over spilt milk" in an attempt to impeach the expert. But the defense attorney did not know how to handle the witness, and the result was devastating:

Q. You said he interpreted the proverb "Crying over spilt milk" correctly that it means "Don't get upset over something you can't change," is that right?

A. Yes.

Q. Wouldn't it be more accurate to say that a correct interpretation would be "Don't get upset over something you have done that you can't change?

A. No.

Q. Okay. Would you feel that the proverb "Don't cry over spilt milk," if you were to say that to a person, it would apply to such things as, we'll say, a person who lives right here in Eugene and has no particular contacts elsewhere in the world, that you would find that comment appropriate if this person you were talking to said, "Wasn't that a terrible thing when that dam went out in Idaho a few weeks ago?"

A. It wouldn't be a normal answer.

Q. No, I don't think so. If a person likewise said, "Isn't it terrible that there is all these international tensions and hijackings, terrorism, things of that sort," would you answer, "But don't cry over spilled milk?"

A. No, I wouldn't.

Q. Okay. Now, my point, doctor, is this: both in your report and on the stand, you said the correct interpretation—and I give the full thing here—"Don't get upset over something you can't change." All I'm pointing out is that is not entirely accurate.

A. Yes, it is.

Q. It would be accurate in some cases, but not always.

A. No, you are wrong.

Q. Okay.

A. That question is off the Wexler Adult Intelligence Scale Test, and his response is right in the main of their appropriate responses for the United States.

Q. Well, how did they determine what an appropriate response is on that test?

A. The same way they standardize that Minnesota Multi-Phasic Personality Inventory with literally thousands of tested situations.

Q. And I assume, then, that in determining what a correct answer is to that proverb was, they did not take into account that at least in some circles, it's been limited to somthing that the person has done, you know, "Don't cry over spilled milk," because you happened to do such-and-such?

A. If you over-personalize the answer like you are trying to do, it is usually in-dicative of a minor thought disorder.

Q. You mean I'm in trouble?

A. Yes, you have got a problem.

Q. Well, at least I found it out free of charge.

A. Nuts!

The astonishing aspect to this dialogue was that after a state's rebuttal witness testified that the defendant had told the witness that he was confi-dent his attorney would get him off, the defense counsel argued to the jury that the defendant must be crazy to have such confidence in his counsel when the evidence showed that his attorney had a problem.

It is important to remember that the psychiatrist is able to testify to everything upon which he based his opinion. This allows the state to in-troduce otherwise inadmissible evidence through the psychiatrist:

> On the other hand, no single act can be of itself decisive; while on the other hand, any act whatever may be significant to some extent. . . The first and fundamental rule, then, will be that *any and all conduct* of the person is ad-missible in evidence. There is no restriction as to the kind of conduct. There can be none; for if a specific act does not indicate insanity, it may indicate sanity.[10]

Diamond and Louisell note, "There is a tendency to hold the prosecution's expert to a more rigid and traditional presentation of his evidence than the witness for the defense."[11] Nevertheless, it is generally admissible to have a psychiatrist testify to all facts upon which he based his opinion.

In addition to a psychiatrist, or in lieu of, the state may also wish to call a clinical psychologist, who may qualify as an expert witness. The Oregon Supreme Court approached this issue in *Sandow* v. *Weyerhaeuser Com-pany*:

> The majority of the available case law indicates that a properly qualified clinical psychologist is competent to testify concerning a person's mental and emotional condition despite his not having medical traning. Though we find no cases which hold that psychologists are competent to testify as to the causative factors of a given mental or emotional condition, the ac-cepted literature in the field of psychology states that such factors are within their expertise.
>
> . . . We hold that clinical psychology has become established and recog-nized as a profession whose members possess special expertise in the field of mental and emotional disorders.[12]

It is imperative, however, that the party calling the witness lay the proper foundation to prove that the witness is qualified to tender an expert opinion. In *Jenkins* v. *United States*, a federal circuit court proposed that the following conditions be satisified:

1. The inferences being drawn must be so related to some science, profession, business or occupation that is sufficiently technical that a lay juror cannot be expected to be equally well qualified to form a worthwhile judgement; and
2. The witness must have such skill, knowledge, or experience in the field or calling in question as to make it appear that his opinion or inference-drawing would probably aid the trier of the facts in his search for truth.[13]

Sandow satisfies the first condition, but the second condition is still an open-ended question in Oregon. An expert witness with a doctorate in clinical psychology and who is licensed to practice in the jurisdiction, has had considerable clinical experience, and has previously testified as an expert witness should qualify as an expert.

A prosecutor who chooses to proceed with an antiexpert expert will have difficulty finding someone willing to accept the mission. Once someone has agreed to serve in this manner, the rest becomes relatively easy. Prosecution and witness should work closely because the expert will be able to supply powerful information with which to impeach the defense expert. He should read through the materials presented in this book, as well as Ziskin's *Coping with Psychiatric and Psychological Testimony*, and all of the investigative material of the particular case.[14] Then prosecutor and witness should prepare a plan to impeach the whole field of psychiatry during all phases of the case. Here, as in other cases, it is sufficiently helpful to warrant the added expense to have the expert listen to as much of the defendant's case as possible. At the least, the witness should be present when the defendant or defendant's expert witnesses testify. Although the court may have ordered witnesses excluded from the courtroom other than when they are testifying, usually it can be argued successfully that the state's expert witness should be permitted to hear the defendant and his experts as a further diagnostic aid. If the expert hears the defense case, the state should try to arrange a break before cross-examination begins so the expert can render invaluable aid in exploiting the weaknesses of the opposing expert's opinion.

In one case, the defendant was charged with possession of marijuana. The case became a crusade by the defendant to legitimize marijuana use based upon supposed religious belief that all "herbs are manna from heaven." Since Oregon case law prohibits a defense to a crime based solely on religious beliefs, the defense attempted to show that the defendant's beliefs about marijuana were delusional and he therefore was not criminally responsible.[15] The state's expert heard the defendant testify, and his opinion was greatly strengthened, he testified, after the defendant's beliefs were scrutinized on cross-examination. Additionally he testified that this was largely because he found the defendant's testimony on direct unbelievable. Thus by having the expert present in court, the prosecutor was able to enhance his expert's credibility and, at the same time, get testimony that the defendant was lying.[16]

The state's attorney should keep a transcript of all expert testimony because it will be confronting psychiatric evidence regularly and will see the same experts repeatedly. Prior transcripts are invaluable because expert witnesses tend to change their reasoning to fit the facts of the particular case.

Notes

1. See J. Ziskin, *Coping with Psychiatric and Psychological Testimony* (Beverly Hills: Law and Psychology Press, 1970).

2. B. Diamond, "The Fallacy of the Impartial Witness," *Archives of Criminal Psychodynamics* 3 (1959): 25.

3. See, *State ex rel. Johnson* v. *Woodrich*, 279 Or. 31, 566 P.2d 859 (1977) and *Shepard* v. *Bowe*, 250 Or. 288, 442 P.2d 238 (1968).

4. *State ex rel. Johnson* v. *Richardson*, 276 Or. 325, 355 SP.2d 202 (1976).

5. *State* v. *Smallwood*, 25 Or. App. 251, 548 P.2d 1346 (1976).

6. *State* v. *Baucom*, 28 Or. App. 757, 561 P.2d 641 (1976).

7. From a staff memorandum from the Multnomah County (Oregon) District Attorney's Office regarding psychiatric defenses. 30 March 1976, p. 6.

8. D. Rosenhan, "On Being Sane in Insane Places," *Science* 179 (1973): 250-258.

9. *State* v. *Ernest Banuelos*, Lane County (Oregon) Circuit Court No. 76-274.

10. John Wigmore, *Evidence* (Boston: Little, Brown, 1940), 2:9.

11. B. Diamond and D. Louisell, "The Psychiatrist as an Expert Witness," *Michigan Law Review* 63 (June 1965): 1352.

12. *Sandow* v. *Weyerhaeuser Company*, 252 Or. 377, 499 P.2d 426 (1969).

13. *Jenkins* v. *United States*, 307 F.2d 637 (D.C. Cir. 1962).

14. Ziskin, *Coping*.

15. See *State* v. *Soto*, 21 Or. App. 794, 537 P.2d 142 (1975).

16. *State* v. *William Conde*, 41 Or. App. 96 (1979).

10 Argument

Traditionally the closing arguments are the most invigorating phase of the case. Every prosecutor has his own approach, but there are certain individual characteristics of an insanity trial that call for a certain response during arguments.

An old rule of thumb was to argue the facts, not the law. This prohibition can be circumvented by saying, "Now the judge will instruct you that . . ." and then stating the law that the state wishes to argue. The insanity defense does require that the law be argued, and many times these cases are tried to the court alone.

The prosecutor must make it clear to the court as well as to the jury that there is a legal test of insanity: that a defendant must (1) have a mental disease or defect, and, as a result thereof, lacks substantial capacity either (2) to appreciate the criminality of his act, or (3) to conform his conduct to the requirements of law. This is crucial because the defendant may appear unbalanced in the courtroom, yet he may not meet the legal test to excuse his conduct. Perhaps his condition has deteriorated since the crime; perhaps he operated under a delusional system but still knew right from wrong and could conform his conduct; or perhaps he is feigning mental illness. Therefore, it is important to explain to the court that the question to be answered is what his mental state was at the time of the crime. The trend with respect to defendants' raising mental defenses is also to make partial responsibility an issue in the case. Thus it is incumbent upon the state to prove that the defendant had the ability to form the intent. This issue must also be clarified for the court. Since these rules of law must be defined for the court (unless the judge is familiar with cases of this sort), the temptation to waive opening argument should be resisted. Otherwise the defense counsel can get the judge off on a tangent that may not relate to the determination that should be made. If the state begins by clarifying the issues and stating the applicable rules of law, the defense attorney will be more apt to confine his argument within the limits and boundaries that have been defined.

In *State* v. *Billy Burnett*, the defendant presented conclusive proof that he was a certified mental retardate.[1] Yet the evidence showed that he could appreciate the criminality of his conduct and could consciously conform his conduct if he so chose. Although the defendant presented evidence of prior adjudications of insanity, the state prevailed because the prosecutor urged the jury to apply the legal formula.

Arguments to the jury must be organized in a slightly different fashion. One school of thought suggests that opening argument be devoted to a discussion of the case on the facts, while closing should concern itself solely with the mental-defense issues. This theory is best used when the defense is claiming that the defendant did not commit the act, but if he did, he was crazy at the time. This method is best applied when the case has been tried by two prosecutors. In *State* v. *Bobby Armstrong*, one prosecutor tried the case in chief and another handled the rebuttal phase (the rebuttal phase was principally concerned with various mental issues).[2] The first prosecutor in opening argument summarized the evidence that tied the defendant to the murder, and the second prosecutor argued the mental issues in closing argument. In opening argument the prosecutor tried to get the defense attorney to commit himself to one theory.

Let's talk about what the defense is in this case. What is the defense? Of course, that's a real problem, isn't it? We don't really know what Mr. M [defense attorney] claims. There are a bunch of different contentions. First of all, that the defendant did not do it and that someone else did it, perhaps a black person, a person with short, curly hair, the person that Mr. K saw. Do you remember him? That was one of Mr. M's witnesses who testified that several of you jurors could be the murderer as far as he knew. And there was another eye witness that Mr. M called that said a black guy did it, not Mr. Armstrong.

The second defense is that Louella M [defendant's girlfriend] did it. There was blood on the side of her coat. Something was brought out that maybe she did it. Mr. M will stand up and argue that Louella did it.

Now, another theory is that it was an accident. The defendant told his mother, a big mistake, "I killed him. Touched the trigger, the gun went off and I ran." Big mistake. Mr. M got the crime lab guy to testify at length about how light the trigger pull is, apparently to substantiate the theory that it might be an accident.

Fourth theory: That he did it, intentionally, but he was under extreme emotional disturbance. Fifth, he got Doctor Bones to say that he did it, but when he did it, he was suffering from a mental disease or defect so that he couldn't appreciate or conform his conduct to the law.

Now I'll bet you that Mr. M won't really commit himself fully to any of those theories. He doesn't want to, and why is that? Why do you have five or six theories if one of them is the truth? You don't, do you? If you had been accused of murder and you felt that you hadn't done it and you went on trial, would you say, "I didn't do it, but if you don't believe that, my girlfriend did it. But if you don't believe that, I was extremely emotionally disturbed, and if you don't believe that, I'm crazy"? Would you do that? No, you wouldn't. Of course not. If your girlfriend did it, you would say, "My girlfriend did it." And if it was an accident, you would say, "It was an accident." If you are crazy, you would say, "I'm crazy." Ask yourself if the defendant looked crazy on the stand. I submit to you, he looked anything but.

I suggest to you that he's got a least five different defenses, because Mr. M knows none of them are worth anything. They are picked out of thin air, put before you in the hopes some of you will like one or more of them and use them as an excuse to let this man off. Of course, that's what Mr. M desires to do. He's employed by the defendant in an ultimate sense and working for his interest, and obviously the defendant's interest in this case is to walk out of here a free man, and Mr. M is trying to do that, isn't he?

The prosecutor's mission in an insanity trial should be to get the defendant to commit himself to one theory during the case. The earlier in the trial that this is done, the better. On the other hand, if the defense refuses to choose until closing argument, the state has already won an important psychological victory in the eyes of the jury. If the defense starts out with two theories and ends up with one, that means that the state has demolished one of them effectively. This will enable the state to argue to the jury that the defense is clutching at any explanation that will exculpate the defendant, and none of its ideas has any merit. It will enable the prosecution to finish with the momentum on its side.

With respect to the divisibility of issues in opening and closing arguments, much can be said for attacking all of the issues in opening argument in order to make the defense attorney respond defensively. Put the opposition on the defensive in voir dire and keep it there through closing argument so that the jury will see the prosecutor as the dominating force. This approach enables the state to argue the burdens of proof more persuasively. If the prosecution has demonstrated to the jury in opening argument that the state has willingly accepted its burden and proved to the jury beyond any doubt that the defendant committed the crime, he can ask the jury, "But what has the defendant done to meet his burden?" This is a good point at which to start attacking psychiatric evidence by showing the speculative nature of the evidence that the defense has advanced to meet its burden. This contrast with the evidence the state has established to prove the crime can only work in its favor.

In *State* v. *Ricky Russell*, the defendant put forth two theories until closing argument. The defendant had sexually assaulted a woman in the city center and claimed (1) that he did not do it for the purpose of sexual arousal and (2) that he was legally insane at the time of the incident. He produced a psychiatrist who testified that the defendant was mentally unfit, but the psychiatrist never bothered to elicit a sexual history from the defendant. In contrast, the state produced an expert who had elicited a sexual history and still could not form an opinion as to the defendant's capacity. In argument, the defense psychiatrist's methods were castigated. By launching a full-scale attack on the psychiatrist, it was argued that the defense had not met its burden because the only evidence it produced was unreliable. Some of that argument follows:

The first question is, does he have a mental disease or defect? According to Dr. H [defense expert], he's a paranoid schizophrenic. Dr. H's testimony, of course, was, "Well, yes, we don't really know how to define paranoid schizophrenia, but we know what it's called."

That is the way that profession bases its determinations. Psychiatrists get together, and they decide by consensus, by voting, whether or not something's a mental disease or defect. And that's how they determine it. Pretty scientific, isn't it? Just by vote.

And that perhaps tells you something about the whole nature of psychiatric and psychological testimony. That it is not a science. That it is somewhat of an art. The art of deciding what is in the human mind. And so anything that these people tell you from the stand has to be taken with those grains of salt. Becuase they cannot predict accurately and definitely whether somebody is sick or not, whether somebody has a mental disease or not. They can only speculate.

Dr. H comes up here and tells you that he knows that there is some doubt in the field, but he's certain of his diagnosis. What did he base it on? He based it primarily on his conversations with the defendant, and he never once asked him for his sexual history. And don't you find that peculiar? That in a crime involving a sexual charge the psychiatrist doesn't even find it relevant to ask the man about his sexual history? And if you recall, I asked the Doctor, well, now, given the fact that there are two stories here, one from the police reports and one from the defendant, don't you find that it might be relevant to see what his sexual history was to determine whether or not he was telling you the truth? Dr. H says, "No, I'm comfortable with my diagnosis, I feel certain of it, I didn't feel that that was relevant." Is that a reasonable way to proceed? Or do you question Dr. H's method of taking information and then making a snap judgment? Is he basing his opinion on any kind of scientific or clinical way of evaluating somebody? Or is he giving his opinion based on his impression? An impression so unfounded in fact, so speculative that he did not even feel it was important to question the defendant about his sexual history.

He even says that the defendant could not appreciate the criminality of his act. That the defendant told him that he knew it was unlawful to touch a woman's breasts, but since the defendant told him that he was only reaching for the victim's necklace he couldn't perceive that as unlawful. Did he ask him if he thought that touching a woman's necklace was unlawful? Wouldn't that help in determining if he could appreciate what was going on? The doctor says, well, that's not relevant. That's not what he's charged with. And I said, well, Doc, what if the defendant could appreciate that it was wrong to go up and touch the woman's necklace, that she had a right not to have him touch it, that it was against the law to physically deal with her in that way. The defendant had been asked that question, and he said, "Yes, I knew that was unlawful. I was taking a risk." The doctor responded, "Well, what he says today doesn't really have much to do with it, does it? He could've improved in jail. And what he's saying today doesn't really have anything to do with what he said on the date of the crime."

And based on that, doesn't that make his whole testimony worthless? Because if he says it doesn't matter what the guy says today, how could it matter what he said to the doctor twenty days after the crime? He doesn't ask the right questions. He doesn't elicit the sexual history. He comes up with a snap judgment. And then he has the audacity to say that what the defendant says to you is irrelevant. And yet isn't his opinion based on what the defendant's telling him? Because certainly he hasn't looked much further. He's got those police reports in front of him. It doesn't seem to make much difference if the defendant told the police that the woman was attractive to him, and that he could understand why she reacted to his assault. Doesn't that show criminality? That he could appreciate that what he did was wrong? Doesn't that show you that he knew what was going on at that time? Well, it may show simple-minded folks like us that, but apparently psychiatrists see things a little differently.

You have all the evidence in front of you. The evidence, I might add, that Dr. H. didn't have in front of him because he didn't care to elicit it. Just because a man's a psychiatrist doesn't mean you have to believe him. The judge will instruct you that the same rules of evidence apply to anyone seated in that witness stand, whether he be defendant, whether he be expert witness, whether he be a police officer.

Let's move on to Dr. K. [state's expert] for a moment. Because you may feel the evidence indicates a contrasting method in the way these two men work. Dr. K. gets up here and says, we ask him what's important in making his determination, and he goes through what he thinks is important. And he says, yes, I've talked to the defendant maybe twenty times, at least four times at length, I examined him for about an hour and a half on this particular case, and how many times has Dr. H. seen him? Once. That's enough for him. And even after seeing the defendant all these different times, and even after eliciting the sexual history from the defendant, which Dr. K. felt was important in making this determination, and even after those particular questions that Dr. H. didn't ask, even after all that evidence, and all the times he saw him, he says, well, what we have is possibilities. "I cannot come to a concrete opinion regarding these things because that would be speculation." And maybe that tells you a little bit about the honesty of that witness. A contrast to Dr. H., who has no trouble giving a seemingly "scientific opinion" about what another witness, a more honest witness, describes as speculation. He says, well, there's possibilities that the defendant could've made all this schizophrenia stuff up after he was in jail. He could've had a sexual urge that was so strong that perhaps it did interfere with his capacity to conform his conduct. And if that were the case, then he would have a defense. Of course on the other hand Dr. K. says he could've had a sexual urge, realizing the behavior was inappropriate, made the decision to go ahead with it anyway, and in that case he could conform his conduct and appreciate the criminality of his act. but chose not to.

And then there's other possibilities, Dr. K. says, there's lots of people who live with delusions, and they can conform their conduct to the requirements of law, they can appreciate the criminality of their acts; and then there are some people who are so delusional that they can't. And he was not able to come to an opinion about whether or not the defendant was so delusional, that he was so out of touch with reality that he couldn't conform his conduct. And that is perhaps significant in this situation, because the defendant, with regards to that portion, has the burden of proof.

The State doesn't have to prove anything to you with regards to the defendant's mental state, because the defendant is presumed sane. Just as he is presumed innocent. And we have to overcome that presumption of innocence with our burden of proof. And the State would submit to you that

that's exactly what has happened. We have proved the facts of this crime
with hard evidence.

The defendant bears the burden of proof to show that he's not responsible,
that he shouldn't be held accountable for this crime. And the State would
submit that he hasn't met that burden. Why hasn't he met that burden?
Because he put on a witness that was so speculative in his testimony, so
dishonest with regard to his conclusions, so incomplete in his analysis, that
that witness was not competent to testify to anything.[3]

Although punishment may not be mentioned during argument, the jury
may already have heard evidence concerning treatment. In *Russell*, both experts spoke of the therapeutic value of incarcerating the defendant. There
are ways to weave these concepts into argument delicately. One tactic is to
alter the terminology. Rather than using words like *insane* or *crazy*, the
defense can be accused of pleading sickness or illness. The state, however, is
not interested in illness; it is interested in accountability and responsibility.
Illnesses may be treated in penitentiary infirmaries. The defense thus can be
exposed as a vehicle for avoiding responsibility. If voir dire went according
to plan, this tactic should strike a responsive chord in the jury box. The jury
should be made aware of the stakes. No juror wants to turn a guilty party
loose, and this sentiment should be utilized. This part of the argument in
Russell is a good example:

And if he made a conscious choice, ladies and gentlemen, then the law does
not excuse his conduct. And in essence, isn't that what he's asking you to
do? He's asking you to free him from criminal responsibility. The defendant in his opening asked you to do justice in this case. The State would
agree. We ask you to do justice. We ask you to hold this man responsible
for the crime that he did in fact commit. He knew what was going on, and
we ask you to find him guilty.

The prosecution should remember to talk about the observations of lay
witnesses. The testimony of experts should not be considered as primary
evidence because they were not eyewitnesses to the crime. In argument the
testimony of eyewitnesses should be reviewed. An advantageous tactic is to
discuss the arrest. If the defendant was able to follow the directives of
police, this fact should be stressed in argument because it shows that the
defendant was able to conform his behavior to the requirements of the law-
enforcement officer. A prosecutor who has been allowed to prove the
defendant's invocation of his *Miranda* rights should comment upon this as
showing his awareness of guilt and thus his responsibility.

Since the prosecutor must prove the facts beyond a reasonable doubt,
the first part of his argument should make it clear to the jury that a crime
was committed by the defendant. Once that reality is established, the
burden shifts psychologically as well as legally. Then he should explain the
mental-defense statute to the jury in order to create a framework from
which he can argue with more clarity. If the jury understands the scope of

the determination initially, the prosecution's argument will not confuse them. He should also analyze the evidence concerning the defendant's mental state.

Argument is perhaps the most personal part of an attorney's case. It is the only time an attorney can demonstrate his own style of dramatic approach. Thus the suggestions in this book are designed only as organizational guidelines.

In a recent case, a successful prosecutor strolled to the blackboard in closing argument and boldly scratched out the words "MUMBO JUMBO" in characterizing the conflicting psychiatric evidence. Sometimes such a device can cut through the fog of nebulous expert testimony and help the jury focus upon the prosecutor's strong hand, the facts of the case.

In *State* v. *Rex Larsen*, the defendant was charged with aggravated murder, rape, sodomy, kidnaping, and other charges.[4] The trial lasted a month, with six psychiatric experts split in their opinions as to whether the defendant was a paranoid schizophrenic who killed as a result of a paranoid delusion or whether he was an antisocial personality who killed the male murder victim in order to molest sexually the victim's girlfriend. All of the psychiatrists agreed that the defendant was criminally responsible for the sex crimes. Under the facts of this case, aggravated murder was the equivalent of a felony murder committed in the course and furtherance of rape and sodomy in the first degree. The prosecution made no mention of the felony-murder doctrine until final argument, when it advised the jurors that if they found that the killing was committed in the course and furtherance of the sex crimes, the defendant would be guilty under the law even if the killing was accidental, or even delusional. The defense counsel vigorously objected, but the court accepted the state's argument that if the defendant had the requisite mental capacity to commit the underlying felonies (and all had agreed he did), then the defendant would be guilty of aggravated (felony) murder if the other elements had been proven.[5] The defense had been caught totally off guard, and it was much too late to do anything about it. It had relied too heavily on its psychiatric evidence and had given too little notice to the way lay jurors would react to the facts. The prosecutor's theory of the murder as being sexually motivated made practical sense; moreover the jury was no longer asked to determine whether the defendant was a paranoid schizophrenic in a delusion, because he was guilty of murder even if he was.

Notes

1. *State* v. *William Burnett*, Lane County (Oregon) Circuit, Court No. 77-1447.

2. *State* v. *Robert Armstrong*, 38 Or. App. 219, 589 P.2d 1174 (1979).

3. *State* v. *Ricky Russell*, Lane County (Oregon) District Court No. 78-170.

4. *State* v. *Rex Larsen*, 44 Or. App. 643 (1980).

5. *State* v. *O'Berry*, 11 Or. App. 552 (1972).

Appendix A:
Case Digest

Mental Disease or Defect

1. *State* v. *Dyer*, 16 Or. App. 247, 514 P.2d 363, 518 P.2d 184 (1974). Defendant was convicted of two counts of murder and one of attempted murder. On appeal the defendant argued that it was error to deny his motion for a mistrial on the basis that the prosecutor used the incorrect insanity test while asking questions of witnesses. The court of appeals reversed the defendant's conviction in its first opinion, but on rehearing en banc, the court concluded that the prosecutor's conduct was not prejudicial error.

The court stated that there are two elements to the new standard of criminal responsibility contained in ORS 161.295(1). The first part of the new test is the functional equivalent of Oregon's former test as enunciated in *State* v. *Gilmore*, 242 Or. 463 (1966). The second part of the test relates only to the defendant's capacity to conform his conduct to the law.

The court concluded by saying that it saw no possibility that the prosecutor's conduct or any other factor in the trial confused the jury into relying upon obsolete law, nor solely upon the cognition element of the new rule of criminal responsibility and ignoring the volition element.

2. *State* v. *Dodson*, 25 Or. App. 859, 551 P.2d 484 (1976). Defendant was convicted of manslaughter. On appeal he argued that the Oregon procedure of placing the burden of proof on defendant on the issue of insanity violated his rights to due process of law.

Held, affirmed. The court stated that Oregon's procedure, which requires that a criminal defendant prove mental disorder or insanity as an affirmative defense, was found to be consistent with due process of law in *Leland* v. *Oregon*, 343 U.S. 790, 72 S.Ct. 1002, 96 L.Ed. 1302 (1951). As a result, defendant's contention on appeal was disregarded.

3. *State* v. *Depue*, 18 Or. App. 158, 524 P.2d 562 (1974). Defendant was convicted of murder. On appeal he contended that the refusal of the trial court to give his requested instruction on mental disease or defect in terms of emotional and intellectual knowledge was reversible error.

Held, affirmed. The court ruled that an instruction on the effect of mental disease or defect in the precise language of the statute governing the effect of mental disease or defect was sufficient.

4. *State* v. *Herrera*, 32 Or. App. 397 (1978). Evidence of drug addiction does not rise to the level of a mental disease or defect, and hence, there was no error when the court refused to give instructions on mental disease as a defense, even though a psychiatrist testified that the defendant probably could not conform his conduct because of the effects of drug addiction.

2. *State* v. *Matthews*, 20 Or. App. 466, 532 P.2d 250 (1975). Defendant's conviction for extreme reckless murder was reversed on appeal. There was some evidence in the record to indicate that because of organic brain damage, defendant's intoxication was involuntary. There also was some evidence to indicate that intoxication combined with organic brain damage allegedly resulted in either a lack of ability to appreciate criminality or to conform conduct.

It was held error for the trial court to exclude testimony on the issue of capacity to conform conduct as a result of intoxication because there was evidence that defendant's drinking was involuntary as opposed to voluntary.

6. *Leland* v. *Oregon*, 343 U.S. 790, 72 S.Ct. 1002 (1951). Defendant was convicted or murder. On appeal to the U.S. Supreme Court, he contended that it was a violation of due process to require him, and not the state, to prove insanity beyond a reasonable doubt.

Held, affirmed. The court held that the Oregon procedure, which requires an accused on a plea of insanity to establish that defense beyond a reasonable doubt, does not violate generally accepted standards of justice and is not in violation of the due-process clause of the U.S. Constitution.

7. *Patterson* v. *N.Y. and U.S.*, 53 L.Ed.2d 281, 97 S.Ct. 2319 (1977). New York State law requires a defendant to prove the affirmative defense of extreme emotional disturbance by a preponderance of the evidence to reduce a charge of second-degree murder to manslaughter. Defendant was convicted of second-degree murder. While his appeal to the U.S. Supreme Court was pending, the Court decided *Mullaney* v. *Wilbur*, 421 U.S. 684, holding that a state must prove all elements of a criminal offense beyond a reasonable doubt and could not constitutionally shift the burden of proving such elements to the defendant.

Defendant's contention on appeal to the Supreme Court was that the *Mullaney* decision rendered the statute under which he was convicted unconstitutional.

Held, affirmed. The New York statute did not violate the due-process clause of the Fourteenth Amendment, since under New York law the affirmative defense in question constituted a separate issue on which the defendant was required to carry the burden of persuasion, and it did not serve to negate any facts of the crime that the state had the burden of proving beyond a reasonable doubt.

8. *Mullaney* v. *Wilbur*, 421 U.S. 684, 95 S.Ct. 1881, 44 L.Ed.2d 508 (1975). Defendant was convicted of murder in Maine. The U.S. Supreme Court held that a murder defendant cannot be required to carry the burden of affirmatively proving heat of passion in order to reduce the crime to manslaughter. The court wrote, "We hold that the due process clause requires the prosecution to prove beyond a reasonable doubt the absence of

the heat of passion or sudden provocation when the issue is properly presented in a homicide case" (421 U.S., at 703-704).

The applicability of this ruling to the burden-of-proof issue in insanity cases is discussed at length in *State* v. *Stockett*, 278 Or. 637. The full opinion in *Stockett* should be consulted on this issue.

Additionally the opinion of Justice Rehnquist in *Mullaney* should be consulted for the reaffirmation of the principle announced in *Leland* v. *Oregon*, 343 U.S. 790, 96 L.Ed. 1302, 72 S.Ct. 1002 (1957), that the placement of the burden of proof on insanity does not result in an unconstitutional shift in the state's traditional burden of proof beyond a reasonable doubt of all elements of an offense.

9. *State ex rel. Johnson* v. *Dale*, 277 Or. 359, 560 P.2d 650 (1977). Defendant was charged with rape and with two counts of sodomy. He pleaded not guilty and gave notice of his intent to rely on the defense of lack of responsibility due to mental disease or defect and on the defense of partial responsibility. The defendant filed a motion to bifurcate the trial. He applied for a jury trial on the issue of guilt or innocence and for a trial before the judge on the issue of his mental responsibility for his acts. The trial court granted his motion.

The Oregon Supreme Court held that the trial court's action in ordering the bifurcated trial for the purpose of avoiding a perceived danger of self-incrimination arising out of a compulsory psychiatric examination constituted an abuse of discretion by the trial court. Additionally the court held that the trial court's action in granting the defendant's motion for a bifurcated trial with separate fact-finders for each part of the trial was beyond any discretion possessed by the trial court under its authority to govern the conduct and procedure of a trial.

10. *State ex rel. Juvenile Department* v. *L.J.*, 26 Or. App. 461, 552 P.2d 1322 (1976). A petition was filed alleging that a fifteen-year-old boy was within the jurisdiction of the juvenile court because of his having committed rape and assault. At his hearing, the juvenile court ruled that he could not raise the defense of mental disease or defect. On appeal the court of appeals held that the ruling of the juvenile court was erroneous and that a juvenile defendant is entitled to the mental-defect defense at a juvenile proceedings.

Diminished or Partial Responsibility

1. *State* v. *Stockett*, 278 Or. 637, 565 P.2d 739 (1977). Defendant was indicted for arson in the first degree and convicted of arson in the second degree. Defendant contended that the trial court erred in refusing to give his requested instruction on diminished intent or partial responsibility under ORS 161.305, and the court of appeals agreed.

On petition for review before the Oregon Supreme Court, the state contended that the trial court's failure to give defendant's requested instruction was not prejudicial and, therefore, was not reversible error.

Held: Revised with directions to reinstate the judgment entered on the jury's verdict. As to the constitutionality of ORS 161.305, the court stated:

> The State contends that if ORS 161.305 is found to be unconstitutional, then the trial court's failure to give defendant's requested instruction wasnot reversible error. The State argues that defendant's requested instruction was an incorrect statement of the law insofar as it instructed the jury in accordance with the terms of ORS 161.305, which we now hold to be unconstitutional." [278 Or. 645]

Hence the partial-responsibility concept is not an affirmative defense, and a defendant who introduces evidence of mental disease or defect under ORS 161.300 is merely attempting to prove that he lacked the requisite mental element.

2. *State* v. *Booth*, 30 Or. App. 351, 567, P.2d 559 (1977). Defendant appealed his conviction for theft. Two expert witnesses testified about his mental aberrations at the time of the theft. The trial court did not instruct the jury on the partial-responsibility doctrine (ORS 161.300), and the defendant contended that the failure to so instruct constituted reversible error.

Held: Conviction affirmed. The Court emphasized four points:

a. ORS 161.300 authorizes any defendant charged with having intentionally done a criminal act as defined in ORS 161.085(7) to introduce the evidence described in ORS 161.300 and to argue to the jury that he was mentally unable to form the intent which is an element of the crime.
b. This is true for any intent crime because there no longer is any specific-intent concept in Oregon criminal law.
c. Subsection 2 is true whether the offense for which defendant is being tried does or does not have lesser included offenses.
d. Instructions to the jury on partial responsibility are not essential since partial responsibility is merely one way for a criminal defendant to confront the state's evidence that he intentionally did a criminal act.

3. *State* v. *Francis*, 30 Or. App. 359, 567 P.2d 558 (1977). Defendant appealed from his conviction for rape, assigning as error the trial court's exclusion of evidence of partial responsibility and failure to instruct on that crime.

Defendant's conviction was affirmed on the basis that the legislative history of ORS 161.300 showed a purposeful decision to limit the admissibility of partial-responsibility evidence to situations where the crime charged included an element of intent. The court declined defendant's invitation to extend ORS 161.300 to crimes involving other mental elements.

4. *State* v. *Schleigh*, 210 Or. 155, 310 P.2d 341 (1957). Defendant was convicted of willfully and maliciously setting a fire. On appeal he contended that it was error for the trial court to refuse to permit the introduction of evidence that he suffered from a mental defect although he failed to give notice of said defense to the court or the district attorney.

The Oregon Supreme Court affirmed his conviction because of the lack of notice of the defense based on mental defect.

Evidence in Insanity Cases

Sufficiency of the Evidence

1. *State* v. *Sands*, 10 Or. App. 438, 499 P.2d 821 (1972). Defendant was convicted of second-degree murder. On appeal he asserted that the evidence established as a matter of law that he was insane at the time of the homicide and that his motion for judgment of acquittal should have been granted.

Held, affirmed. The court looked to the whole record, including the evidence introduced and the reasonable inferences that could be drawn therefrom, and it concluded that reasonable people could differ on defendant's mental state and, therefore, the question was for the trier of fact.

2. *State* v. *Smith*, 21 Or. App. 270, 534 P.2d 1180 (1975). Defendant was convicted of attempted murder and assault in the second degree. On appeal he contended that he had met his burden of proof on the issue of mental disease or defect and that the court should have ruled that as a matter of law he had sustained his burden since the state allegedly failed to present any rebuttal evidence.

Held, affirmed. Although evidence of insanity can be so substantial that the matter should be withdrawn from the jury and decided favorably to the defendant, the court found that there was significant evidence to show defendant was acting rationally. Since reasonable people could differ on defendant's mental state, the issue was properly left to the jury.

3. *State* v. *Rainwater*, 26 Or. App. 593, 553 P.2d 1085 (1976). Defendant was convicted of assault in the first degree but was acquitted of two counts of attempted murder pursuant to his plea of not guilty by reason of mental disease or defect. On appeal, defendant contended that his conviction of the lesser included crimes of assault were improper since the court specifically found that he lacked the capacity to appreciate the criminality of his conduct with respect to the greater crimes charged.

Held, reversed. The defendant's initial action of firing a random shot before losing control of himself could not support an assault conviction because there was no evidence of physical injury to either victim. However, the court held that since the defendant's conduct clearly could be found to constitute the lesser included offense of menacing or recklessly endangering, he could be sentenced on these charges, notwithstanding his defense of mental disease or defect.

The court noted that there was ample evidence to support the conclusion that defendant had the requisite mental capacity to commit an assault when he first fired the shot. Where the evidence provides a reasonable basis for a finding that a continuing course of criminal conduct is divisible, a conviction for the initially committed offense is permissible even though a defendant may thereafter lack the capacity to commit the remaining crimes.

Presumptions

Although the general rule is that all persons are presumed sane, the following cases illustrate that in some situations, the opposite presumption applies. Currently this area of Oregon law is a topic of much debate and potentially subject to revision in the near future.

1. *State* v. *Garver*, 190 Or. 291, 225 P.2d 771 (1950). Murder conviction reversed for failure to give instruction that the law presumes that insanity, having once been shown to exist, continues until contrary is made to appear. The supreme court decided that when permanent, chronic, or continuous insanity is proved to have existed at some time prior to the alleged crime, it will be presumed to continue. This presumption arises especially upon proof of a prior adjudication of insanity. No such presumption arises from proof of a prior insane condition that was merely temporary in character.

2. *State* v. *Porter*, 29 Or. App. 67, 564 P.2d 1104 (1977). Defendant appealed his burglary conviction for failure of the trial court to grant judgment of acquittal on the ground that the state's evidence failed to overcome a presumption of continuing insanity. The court of appeals rejected defendant's contention, holding that the testimony of lay witnesses established that defendant seemed calm and in good composure, spoke slowly and clearly, and did not appear to be nervous. It wrote, "This evidence, if believed by the trial judge—as it was—was sufficient to overcome the disputable presumption of continuing insanity."

3. *State* v. *Weller*, 32 Or. App. 619, 574 P.2d 1144 (1978). Defendant appealed theft conviction contending that it was error to refuse to instruct the jury that insanity, having once been shown to exist, is presumed to continue until the contrary is shown. Defendant had been committed previously to the Oregon state hospial as a chronic paranoid schizophrenic. The trial judge rejected the instruction because it used language borrowed from the pre-1971 statute; as such, it was an incorrect statement of the law. The court of appeals affirmed the conviction. The court made this comment on *State* v. *Garver* in its decision:

The court in *Garver*, which was an extreme case and involved the death penalty, specifically stated that it was more inclined to require that the instruction be given because of the harshness of the statute that required defendant to prove his insanity beyond a reasonable doubt. *State of Oregon* v. *Garver*, *supra* at 308. In 1977 defendant was only required to prove by a preponderance of the evidence that he suffered from a mental disease or defect.

In view of the changes in the law since *Garver* was decided and because we feel the requested instruction would have been misleading, we hold that the trial court properly refused the requested instruction.

Expert Witnesses

1. *State* v. *Baucom*, 28 Or. App. 757, 561 P.2d 641 (1977). Defendant was convicted of first-degree assault. On appeal defendant argued that the court improperly excluded the testimony of a psychiatric social worker as to whether the defendant was suffering from a mental disease or defect at the time he committed the assault. Defendant also argued that the trial court improperly admitted the testimony of a state's psychiatrist who examined him without first giving the defendant adequate *Miranda* warnings.

Held, affirmed. The court ruled that the psychiatric social worker who counseled the defendant after the offense was not competent to give expert testimony because her work did not encompass making retrospective diagnoses of the existence of a mental disease or defect, an admission that she was not "a person skilled touching the matter of inquiry." As to the inadequacy of the *Miranda* warnings, the court ruled that the defendant was not prejudiced thereby.

2. *Tarasoff* v. *Regents of University of California*, 131 Cal. Rptr. 14, 551 P.2d 334 (1976). An action was brought against university regents and psychotherapists employed by the university hospital to recover for murder of the plaintiff's daughter by a psychiatric patient.

The California Supreme Court held that the University of California, as an employer of treating and supervising psychotherapists, could be held liable for the therapist's breach of duty to exercise reasonable care to protect the plaintiff's decedent from danger posed by a mental patient who allegedly confided to the therapists his intentions to kill the plaintiff's daughter.

When a psychotherapist determines, or pursuant to the standards of his profession should determine, that his patient presents a serious danger of violence to another, he incurs an obligation to use reasonable care to protect the intended victim against such danger. To discharge this obligation, a therapist must take affirmative action to protect the foreseeable victim of that danger.

3. *State* v. *Nulph*, 31 Or. App. 1155, 572 P.2d 642 (1977). The trial court properly excluded evidence of a defense psychiatrist's interview with the defendant while the defendant was under the influence of sodium amitol. See also *State* v. *Harris*, 241 Or. 224, 405 P.2d 492 (1965), excluding use of an interview conducted while defendant was under hypnosis.

4. *State* v. *Eichenberger*, 25 Or. App. 499, 549 P.2d 1300 (1976). Defendant was convicted of murder. Defendant's argument on appeal was that a psychiatrist was permitted to testify concerning his statements about the crime, even though the doctor had not advised the defendant of his *Miranda* rights.

Held, affirmed. The court found that the *Corbin* rule was not applicable here because the psychiatrist who examined the defendant was not employed by the state as an adversary: "Although Dr. Weissert was employed by defendant's adversary in the sense of being a public employee, we hold that he was, for present purposes, defendant's own doctor" (25 Or. App. at 510).

5. *State* v. *Corbin*, 15 Or. App. 536, 516 P.2d 1314 (1973). The court of appeals also ruled that a defendant must be warned prior to a psychiatric examination that he has the right to refuse to talk to the state's psychiatrist who examines him, since he is an officer of the state and is no different from any police officer questioning a defendant. Thus a valid consent to a psychiatric examination may not be obtained without defendant's knowingly and voluntarily waiving his right to remain silent and his right to counsel.

6. *State* v. *Smallwood*, 25 Or. App. 251, 548 P.2d 1346 (1976). Defendant was convicted of murder in Multnomah County. Defendant's assignment of error asserted violation of his Fifth Amendment rights in connection with certain testimony elicited from the state's psychiatrist.

Held, affirmed. The court distinguished *Shepherd* v. *Bowe*, in holding that a state psychiatrist was properly permitted to testify that the defendant asserted his Fifth and Sixth amendment rights by refusing to answer certain questions during the interview. Following the testimony of the defendant and his psychiatrist, the state's psychiatrist was allowed to explain to the jury that defendant had refused to talk with him without his attorney present, and when the attorney was present had refused to discuss the alleged crime.

7. *State* v. *Smallwood*, 277 Or. 503, 561 P.2d 600 (1977). On review the supreme court affirmed the decision of the court of appeals, finding that "in view of the circumstances, we believe there was no real likelihood that any adverse inferences were drawn by the jury from defendant's assertion of his right not to talk about the details of the killing." This decision somewhat limits the court of appeals's decision in that the supreme court impliedly indicates that if a psychiatrist is allowed to testify about a defen-

dant's invocation of his constitutional rights, it may raise a *Griffin* v. *California*, 380 U.S. 609, 85 S.Ct. 1229 (1965), problem depending on the circumstances.

8. *Shepherd* v. *Bowe*, 250 Or. 288, 442 P.2d 238 (1968). The issue presented was the extent of the pretrial psychiatric examination that a trial court can require of a defendant who has pleaded not guilty by reason of insanity.

The supreme court held that the trial court was without authority to require that a defendant at the pretrial mental examination answer questions concerning his conduct relating to the offense charged and could not order defendant's counsel not to advise his client to refuse to answer questions on the ground that they might incriminate him. Thus a defendant must be advised of his *Miranda* rights before questioning by a state's psychiatrist.

9. *State ex rel. Johnson* v. *Richardson*, 276 Or. 325, 555 P.2d 202 (1976). Defendant was charged with a crime and gave notice of his intent to rely upon the defense of mental defect. The state moved for an order requiring defendant to submit to a psychiatric examination. Defendant filed an affidavit stating that unless ordered by the court, he would not answer any questions asked of him by the psychiatrist. At this time the state moved for an order requiring the defendant to answer questions "other than [concerning] acts or conduct immediately near the scene of the crime." The trial court denied the latter motion, and the state petitioned for a writ of mandamus.

Held, writ allowed. The court distinguished *Shepherd* v. *Bowe* and concluded that the defendant should be required to answer questions not pertaining to the commission of the crime, and that if he continued to refuse, his affirmative defense of mental defect would be stricken. The danger that answers to questions posed by the psychiatrist may indirectly lead to evidence tending to incriminate the defendant was found to be insufficient to authorize the defendant not to answer the questions.

10. *State* v. *Phillips*, 245 Or. 466, 422 P.2d 670 (1967). Defendant, convicted of first-degree murder, appealed. On appeal the court held that when a defendant pleads not guilty by reason of insanity, the state is entitled to have the defendant submit to a mental examination. The court wrote, "If the rule were otherwise, there would be no way for the state to rebut a plea of insanity after the defendant had put his mental condition in question by such a plea" (245 Or. at 476).

11. *State ex rel. Johnson* v. *Woodrich*, 279 Or. 31, 566 P.2d 859, (1977). Defendant was charged with murder and felony murder and gave notice of his intent to raise the defense of mental disease or defect and to introduce evidence of extreme emotional disturbance. The state moved for an order allowing state psychiatrists to examine the defendant. In accordance with *Shepherd* v. *Bowe*, 250 Or. 288, the trial court did not permit inquiry

into acts or conduct at or immediately near the time of the commission of the alleged crimes. The state contended that the judge has the duty to order a complete psychiatric examination.

Held: The trial judge correctly followed the holding of *Shepherd* v. *Bowe* in limiting the scope of compulsory pretrial psychiatric examination. The state's writ of mandamus was denied.

A strong dissent was filed by Judge Howell, who believed that when a defendant raises the insanity defense, the state's psychiatrist should be allowed to conduct a complete examination of the defendant.

12. *State* v. *Akridge*, 23 Or. App. 733, 543 P.2d 1073 (1975). The court of appeals held that the trial court did not err in allowing the state to exercise its statutory right to compel the defendant to submit to a psychiatric examination even though the trial had begun.

13. *State* v. *Wampler*, 30 Or. App. 936, 569 P.2d 46 (1977). Defendant was convicted of murder and contended on appeal that certain videotaped psychiatric examinations should not have been admitted. In affirming, the appellate court stated:

> Defendant contends that the trial court erred in permitting the prosecution to introduce two videotapes of defendant's psychiatric examinations. The tapes were made at defendant's request to assist the psychiatrists in their diagnoses of defendant's mental condition. The prosecution initially objected to the making of the videotapes. The trial court did not rule on the admissibility of the tapes until they were offered at trial by the prosecution. Defendant argues that because the State initially opposed the making of the tapes, it should have been stopped from offering them into evidence. We are aware of no such rule; we perceive no valid reason for adopting such a theory and we decline to do so.

> Defendant also contends that the videotapes were inadmissible for the following reasons: defendant was not given *Miranda* warnings prior to the commencement of the examinations; the psychiatrists questioned defendant about his exercise of his *Miranda* rights shortly after the murder; and had defendant known that the videotapes would be admitted at trial, he may have exercised his right to have counsel present and his right not to respond to questions concerning the criminal event.

> In view of the fact that defendant admitted the shooting at trial, that the interviews were conducted and videotaped at the behest of defense counsel, and that defense counsel was fully aware that he could be present at the examinations and that his client could decline to answer questions regarding the shooting, we hold that the videotapes were not rendered inadmissible on any of these grounds.

14. *State* v. *Glover*, 33 Or. App. 553, 577 P.2d 91 (1978). Held: (1) Defendant is not entitled to have the state furnish another psychiatrist selected by him when the psychiatrist already provided gave defendant adequate means to prepare and present affirmative defense. (2) The court was

not in error in refusing to discharge defendant's court-appointed attorney because defendant was competently and ably represented, and interests of justice did not require substitution.

15. *State* v. *Goss*, 33 Or. App. 507, 577 P.2d 78 (1978). Defendant admitted killing the gas-station attendant but relied on mental disease or defect defense. At trial state's witnesses testified that defendant planned to blow up a building to earn $500 and had smoked and sold marijuana in the past.

Held: Evidence that defendant planned to blow up a building was an integral part of the history that the expert relied on in making his diagnosis and is therefore admissible. Evidence concerning marijuana had no relevance as to defendant's mental state, but error was not prejudicial.

16. *State* v. *Girard*, 34 Or. App. 85, 578 P.2d 415 (1978). Defendant was convicted of burglary, escape, and assault. The trial judge excluded testimony of defendant's psychiatrist regarding statements made by defendant to the psychiatrist during his examination of defendant.

Held, error. The psychiatrist should have been allowed to relate defendant's statements of his medical history and his history concerning drinking and drug abuse since these factors were relevant to the diagnosis.

17. *State* v. *Massey*, 34 Or. App. 95, 577 P.2d 1364 (1978). Defendant was convicted of manslaughter. At trial, certain evidence of social and medical history of the defendant and the victim was excluded. The evidence excluded consisted of boys' ranch and army records of defendant and the diary and medical records of the victim. Defendant's psychiatrist claimed that the defendant's records supported his conclusion that defendant had decompensated into a psychotic state on the night of the killing. He also claimed that the victim's records and diary demonstrated that the victim was suffeirng from severe mental problems, which caused the stress in defendant necessary to bring about defendant's decompensation and loss of control.

Held, reversed. It was within the court's discretion to exclude defendant's records, since their probative value was outweighed by policy considerations such as confusion of the jury and undue consumption of time. The victim's records should have been admitted. They made defendant's theory more plausible, and there was no detailed testimony as to the contents of the exhibits. Defendant's doctor was allowed only to state that he had relied on the exhibits, and the jury was thus deprived of hearing his theory about how the victim's mental state had precipitated defendant's mental decompensation.

Qualification of Lay Witness to Testify

1. *State* v. *Van Dolah*, 14 Or. App. 125, 512 P.2d 1013 (1973). Defendant was convicted of third-degree rape. His contention on appeal was that it

was error for the trial court to permit lay witnesses to express opinions concerning the defendant's sanity.

Held, affirmed. The court relied on ORS 41.900(10) in ruling that witnesses who are intimately acquainted with a criminal defendant may express opinions concerning a defendant's sanity:

Evidence may be given of the following facts:

. . . the opinion of an intimate acquaintance respecting the mental sanity of a person, the reason for the opinion being given. [ORS 41.900(10)]

2. *State* v. *Sands*, 10 Or. App. 438, 499 P.2d 821 (1972). Defendant was convicted of second-degree murder. The only expert witness was called by the defendant. On appeal he asserted that this evidence established as a matter of law that he was insane at the time of the crime.

Held, affirmed. The evidence was sufficient to submit the question of the defendant's sanity to the jury. The jury was not required to believe the expert's testimony. However, the court did rule that the evidence of insanity can be so substantial that the matter should be withdrawn from the trier of fact and be decided favorably to the defendant by the trial judge as a matter of law. Here there was other evidence that defendant behaved in a rational and coherent manner.

3. *State* v. *Dyer*, 16 Or. App. 247, 514, P.2d 363, 518 P.2d 184 (1974). Defendant assigned as error the testimony of certain lay witnesses concerning the defendant's sanity at the time of the murders.

The court held that it is within the discretion of the trial court to say when the witness has shown himself to be competent and qualified to express an opinion upon the subject at issue. Here, the lay witnesses who expressed their opinions as to the defendant's sanity were found to be sufficiently intimate with the defendant to testify.

4. *State* v. *Fowler*, 37 Or. App. 299 (1978). Defendant was convicted of armed robbery. On appeal he claimed that defendant's former probation officer should have been allowed to give opinion testimony as to defendant's sanity.

Held, affirmed. Witness was not an "intimate acquaintance" under ORS 41.900(10) since he had not met defendant for over seven months, and prior to that had met with defendant only for ten to twenty minutes twice a month.

Defendant's Invocation of Constitutional Rights

1. *State* v. *McCauley*, 8 Or. App. 571, 494 P.2d 438 (1972). Defendant was convicted of manslaughter and argued on appeal that it was error to permit

testimony of a police officer that defendant had invoked his Sixth Amendment right to remain silent upon arrest.

In affirming, the court ruled:

> He asserted the defense of insanity. His remarks to the officer were made shortly after his wife had died and were relevant to show his understanding and comprehension of what took place at the time of the stabbing. The circumstances surrounding his making those voluntary remarks were also relevant to that issue. [8 Or. App. at 577)

In *State* v. *Nulph*, 31 Or. App. 1155, 572 P.2d 642 (1977), however, the court held it harmless error to permit the police officer to testify that defendant had told him, "I'd better talk to a lawyer." The court distinguished the situation where defendant maintains innocence for the crime, as here, while also raising a mental defense, as opposed to the case where the defendant admits the crime and relies only upon a mental defense as in *McCauley* and *Smallwood*.

2. *State* v. *Reid*, 36 Or. App. 417, 585 P.2d 411 (1978). Defendant was convicted of burglary. At trial, evidence was admitted that after defendant was arrested, he told the officer he would not talk because anything he said could be used against him.

Held, affirmed. Defendant raised a mental defense. The state was entitled to rebut any inferences the jury would draw respecting defendant's mental condition by showing he acted rationally within a few minutes after the crime was committed.

Extreme Emotional Disturbance

1. *State* v. *McCoy*, 17 Or. App. 155, 521 —.2d 1074 (1974). Defendant was found guilty of murder. On appeal defendant argued that in order to be convicted of murder, the jury must find beyond a reasonable doubt that the defendant was not suffering from an extreme emotional disturbance at the time of the killing.

The court in affirming defendant's conviction held that the state has the burden of persuasion on the issue of extreme emotional disturbance and that the jury should be instructed that to convict the defendant of murder, it must find beyond a reasonable doubt the nonexistence of extreme emotional disturbance.

2. *State* v. *Corbin*, 15 Or. App. 536, 516 P.2d 1314 (1973). Defendant was convicted of murder. On appeal defendant contended that an instruction given to the jury to the effect that the defense of extreme emotional disturbance requires that there be both an "unexpected and provocative event which triggered the defendant into committing the homicide" was erroneous.

In reversing defendant's conviction, the court held that the issue of whether there was reasonable explanation for the emotional disturbance of defendant was to be determined by the jury and that the defense of extreme emotional disturbance is not limited to cases involving unexpected or provocative events.

3. *State* v. *Keys*, 25 Or. App. 15, 548 P.2d 205 (1976). Defendant demurred to an indictment alleging that he did "unlawfully and intentionally cause the death of another human being" on the ground that it failed to allege that he was not under the influence of an extreme emotional disturbance. ORS 163. 115(1)(a). The trial court ruled that extreme emotional disturbance must be negated in every murder indictment.

On appeal by the State, the court reversed and held:

a.   Extreme emotional disturbance need not be negated in a murder indictment.
b.   Extreme emotional disturbance is not to be labeled a defense in the technical sense requiring the state to negate it if pretrial notice of reliance is given by the defense. This ruling was seen as contrary to the interpretation given in *State* v. *McCoy*.
c.   Extreme emotional disturbance becomes an issue in a murder prosecution when there is evidence at trial that raises it. This evidence can be either the state's or the defendant's.

4. *State* v. *Akridge*, 23 Or. App. 633, 543 P.2d 1073 (1975). Defendant was convicted of murder and appealed. The contention raised by defendant on appeal was that the trial court incorrectly instructed the jury on the phrase *extreme emotional disturbance*. The court's instruction stated in part that "in determining what the term 'extreme' means with reference to extreme emotional disturbance, I instruct you that the term means the outermost or furthest; most remote in any direction; final; or last."

Held: Affirmed. The court stated that in absence of any statutory definition of *extreme* or *emotional disturbance*, the trial court correctly used the customary meaning of the word in instructing on extreme emotional disturbance.

5. *State* v. *Davis*, 16 Or. App. 405, 518 P.2d 1039 (1974). Defendant was convicted of murder. On appeal he contended that the defense of extreme emotional disturbance should have mitigated murder to manslaughter (ORS 161.125(1)(b)).

Held, conviction affirmed. The court of appeals reaffirmed its rulings in *State* v. *Siens*, 12 Or. App. 97 (1973), that the decision as to the reasonableness of the explanation for the extreme emotional disturbance is entirely in the hands of the jury.

6. *State* v. *Seins*, 12 Or. App. 9975, 504l P.2d 1056 (1973). Defendant was convicted of two murders. At trial, defendant's counsel moved for re-

moval of the charge of murder from consideration by the jury because the state had failed to prove beyond a reasonable doubt that the defendant was not suffering from extreme emotional disturbance.

Held: Affirmed. The court held that extreme emotional disturbance is a defense, not an affirmative defense, under the criminal code. As a result, the state has the burden of disproving the defense beyond a reasonable doubt. Here the court felt that there was adequate evidence offered by the state that defendant was not under the influence of extreme emotional disturbance at the time of the shootings.

Appendix B:
Statutory Guide

In 1977 the Oregon legislature revised the statutory scheme regarding the responsibility defense statutes. The significant changes are that (1) the verdict form has been changed from "not guilty by reason of mental disease or defect" to "not responsible by reason of mental disease or defect" pursuant to revised ORS 161.295, 161.319, 161.325; and (2) a psychiatric-review board has been established to govern the release of persons adjudicated not responsible after they have been committed to state mental hospitals (ORS 161.336).

The adoption of the psychiatric-review board has been received with mixed emotion. Some see it as a way of providing a stable approach to the supervision and release of dangerous individuals. Others see it somewhat to the contrary, since the psychiatric review board operates in Salem, the state capitol, and is somewhat removed from, and hence unaccountable to, the community to which most individuals will be released. Moreover, the review board will not be as familiar with the original facts that led to the person's commitment, as would the committing judge.

The responsibility statutes, which begin with ORS 161.295 and end with ORS 161.395, are reprinted here.

161.295 *Effect of mental disease or defect.* (1) A person is not responsible for criminal conduct if at the time of such conduct as a result of mental disease or defect he lacks substantial capacity either to appreciate the criminality of his conduct or to conform his conduct to the requirements of law.

(2) As used in chapter 743, Oregon Laws 1971, the terms "mental disease or defect" do not include an abnormality manifested only by repeated criminal or otherwise antisocial conduct.

161.300 *Evidence of disease or defect admissible as to intent.* Evidence that the actor suffered from a mental disease or defect is admissible whenever it is relevant to the issue of whether he did or did not have the intent which is an element of the crime.

161.305 *Disease or defect as affirmative defense.* Mental disease or defect excluding responsibility under ORS 161.295 or partial responsibility under ORS 161.300 is an affirmative defense.

161.309 *Notice prerequisite to defense; content.* (1) No evidence may be introduced by the defendant on the issue of criminal responsibility as defined in ORS

161.295, unless he gives notice of his intent to do so in the manner provided in subsection (3) of this section.

(2) The defendant may not introduce in his case in chief expert testimony regarding partial responsibility under ORS 161.300 unless he gives notice of his intent to do so in the manner provided in subsection (3) of this section.

(3) A defendant who is required under subsection (1) or (2) of this section to give notice shall file a written notice of his purpose at the time he pleads not guilty. The defendant may file such notice at any time after he pleads but before trial when just cause for failure to file the notice at the time making his plea is made to appear to the satisfaction of the court. If the defendant fails to file any such notice, he shall not be entitled to introduce evidence for the establishment of a defense under ORS 161.295 or 161.300 unless the court, in its discretion, permits such evidence to be introduced where just cause for failure to file the notice is made to appear.

161.315 *Right of state to obtain mental examination of defendant; limitations.* Upon filing of notice or the introduction of evidence by the defendant as provided in subsection (3) of ORS 161.309, the state shall have the right to have at least one psychiatrist or licensed psychologist of its selection examine the defendant. The state shall file notice with the court of its intention to have the defendant examined. Upon filing of the notice, the court, in its discretion, may order the defendant committed to a state institution or any other suitable facility for observation and examination as it may designate for a period not to exceed 30 days. If the defendant objects to the examiner chosen by the state, the court for good cause shown may direct the state to select a different examiner.

161.319 *Form of verdict on acquittal on grounds of disease or defect.* When the defendant is found not responsible due to mental disease or defect, as defined in ORS 161.295, the verdict and judgment shall so state.

161.325 *Entry of order finding defendant not responsible on grounds of disease or defect.* After entry of judgment of not responsible due to mental disease or defect, the court shall, on the basis of the evidence given at the trial or at a separate hearing, if requested by either party, make an order as provided in ORS 161.329, 161.336 or 161.341, whichever is appropriate. If the court makes an order as provided in ORS 161.336, it shall also determine on the record what offense the person would have been convicted of had the person been found responsible.

161.329 *Order of conditional release.* If the court finds that the person is no longer affected by mental disease or defect, or, if so affected, that he no longer represents a substantial danger to himself or others and is ot in need of care, supervision or treatment, the court shall order him discharged from custody.

161.332 *Definition of conditional release.* As used in ORS 137.540, 161.315, 161.351, 161.385 to 161.395, 192.690 and 428.210, "conditional release" includes, but is not limited to, the monitoring of mental and physical health treatment.

161.336 *Order giving jurisdiction to Psychiatric Security Review Board; board determination and designation; supervision by board; application for modification of board order.* (1) Following the entry of a judgment pursuant to ORS 161.319, if the court finds by a preponderance of the evidence that the person is affected by mental disease or defect and that he presents a substantial danger to himself or others that requires that the person be committed to a stated mental hospital designated by the Mental Health Division or conditionally released, the court shall order him placed under the jurisdiction of the Psychiatric Security Review Board for care and treatment. The period of jurisdiction of the board shall be equal to the maximum sentence the court finds the person could have received had he been found responsible. The board shall hold a hearing within 20 days to determine whether the person should be committed or conditionally released. Pending hearing before the board, the person may be committed to a state hospital designated by the Mental Health Division.

(2) If the board determines that the person presents a substantial danger to himself or others but that he can be adequately controlled with supervision and treatment if he is conditionally released and that necessary supervision and treatment is available, the board may order him conditionally released, subject to those supervisory orders of the board as are in the best interests of justice, the protection of society and the welfare of the person. The board may designate any person or state, county or local agency the board considers capable of supervising the person upon release, subject to those conditions as the board directs in the order for conditional release. Prior to the designation, the board shall notify the person or agency to whom conditional release is contemplated and provide the person or agency an opportunity to be heard before the board. After receiving an order entered under this section, the person or agency designated shall assume supervision of the person pursuant to the direction of the board.

(3) Conditions of release contained in orders entered under this section may be modified from time to time and conditional releases may be terminated by order of the board as provided in ORS 161.351.

(4) For purposes of this section, a person affected by a mental disease or defect in a state of remission is considered to have a mental disease or defect requiring supervision when his disease may, with reasonable medical probability, occasionally become active and, when active, render him a danger to himself or others. The person may be continued on conditional release by the board as provided in this section.

(5) (a) As a condition of release, the board may require the person to report to any state or local mental health facility for evaluation. Whenever medical, psychiatric or psychological treatment is recommended, the board may order the person, as a condition of release, to cooperate with and accept the treatment from the facility.

(b) The facility to which the person has been referred for evaluation shall perform the evaluation and submit a written report of its findings to the board. If the facility finds that treatment of the person is appropriate, it shall include its recommendation for treatment in the report to the board.

(c) Whenever treatment is provided by the facility, it shall furnish reports to the board on a regular basis concerning the progress of the person.

(d) Copies of all reports submitted to the board pursuant to this section shall be furnished to the person and his counsel. The confidentiality of these reports shall be determined pursuant to ORS 192.500.

(e) The facility shall comply with any other conditions of release prescribed by the board.

(6) If at any time while the person is under the jurisdiction of the board it appears to the board or its chairman that the person has violated the terms of the conditional release or that the mental health of the individual has changed, the board or its chairman may order the person returned to a state hospital designated by the Mental Health Division for evaluation or treatment. Within 20 days of a revocation of a conditional release, the board shall conduct a hearing. Notice of the hearing shall be given to the person, the court and the district attorney from the committing county of the time and place of the hearing. The board may continue the person on conditional release or, if it finds by a preponderance of the evidence that the person is affected by mental disease or defect and presents a substantial danger to himself or others and cannot be adequately controlled if conditional release is continued, it may order the person committed to a state hospital designated by the Mental Health Division. The State must prove by a preponderance of the evidence the person's unfitness for conditional release. A person in custody pursuant to this subsection shall have the same rights as any person appearing before the board pursuant to ORS 161.346.

(7) The community mental health program director, the director of the facility providing treatment to a person on conditional release, any peace officer or any person responsible for the supervision of a person on conditional release may take a person on conditional release into custody or request that the person be taken into custody if he has reasonable cause to believe the person is a substantial danger to himself or others because of mental disease or defect and that the person is in need of immediate care, custody or treatment. Any person taken into custody pursuant to this subsection shall immediately be transported to a state hospital designated by the Mental Health Division. A person taken into custody under this subsection shall have the same rights as any person appearing before the board pursuant to ORS 161.346.

(8) (a) Any person conditionally released under this section may apply to the board for discharge from or modification of an order of conditional release on the ground that he is no longer affected by mental disease or defect or, if still so affected, no longer presents a substantial danger to himself or others and he no longer requires supervision, medication, care or treatment. Notice of the hearing on an application for discharge or modification of an order of conditional release shall be made to the district attorney and the court or department of the county of original

commitment. The applicant must prove by a preponderance of the evidence his fitness for discharge or modification of the order of conditional release. Applications by the person for discharge or modification of conditional release shall not be filed more often than once every six months.

(b) Upon application by any person or agency responsible for supervision or treatment pursuant to an order of conditional release, the board shall conduct a hearing to determine if the conditions of release shall be continued, modified or terminated. The application shall be accompanied by a report setting forth the facts supporting the application.

(9) The total period of conditional release and commitment ordered pursuant to this section shall not exceed the maximum sentence the person could have received had he been found responsible.

(10) The board shall maintain and keep current the medical, social and criminal history of all persons committed to its jurisdiction. The confidentiality of records maintained by the board shall be determined pursuant to ORS 192.500.

(11) In determining whether a person should be committed to a state hospital, conditionally released or discharged, the board shall have as its primary concern the protection of society.

161.341 *Order of commitment; application for discharge or conditional release.* (1) If the board finds that the person presents a substantial danger to himself or others and that he is not a proper subject for conditional release, the board shall order him committed to a state hospital designated by the Mental Health Division for custody, care and treatment. The period of commitment ordered by the board shall not exceed the maximum sentence the person could have received had he been found responsible.

(2) If at any time after the commitment of a person to a state hospital designated by the Mental Health Division under this section, the superintendent of the hospital is of the opinion that the person is no longer affected by mental disease or defect, or, if so affected, that he no longer presents a substantial danger to himself or others or that the person continues to be affected by mental disease or defect and continues to be a danger to himself or others, but that the person can be controlled with proper care, medication, supervision and treatment if conditionally released, the superintendent shall apply to the board for an order of discharge or conditional release. The application shall be accompanied by a report setting forth the facts supporting the opinion of the superintendent. Within 30 days of the hearing before the board, copies of the report shall be sent to the district attorney and the circuit court or department of the county of original commitment. The district attorney or circuit court or department of the county shall notify the board in writing if they wish to present evidence at the hearing.

(3) The district attorney or circuit court or department of the county from which the person was committed may choose a psychiatrist or licensed psychologist to ex-

amine the person prior to a decision by the board on discharge or conditional release. The results of the examination shall be in writing and filed with the board, and shall include, but need not be limited to, an opinion as to the mental condition of the person, whether the person presents a substantial danger to himself or to others, and whether the person could be adequately controlled with treatment as a condition of release.

(4) Any person who has been committed to a state hospital designated by the Mental Health Division for custody, care and treatment or another person acting on his behalf, after the expiration of six months from the date of the order of commitment, may apply to the board for an order of discharge or conditional release upon the grounds:

(a) That he is no longer affected by mental disease or defect;

(b) If so affected, that he no longer presents a substantial danger to himself or others; or

(c) That he continues to be affected by a mental disease or defect and would continue to be a danger to himself or others without treatment, but he can be adequately controlled and given proper care and treatment if placed on conditional release.

(5) When application is made under subsection (4) of this section, the board shall require a report from the superintendent of the hospital which shall be prepared and transmitted as provided in subsection (2) of this section. The applicant must prove by a preponderance of the evidence his fitness for discharge under the standards of subsection (4) of this section. Applications for discharge or conditional release under subsection (4) of this section shall not be filed more often than once every six months.

(6) In no case shall a person be held pursuant to this section for a period of time exceeding two years without a hearing before the board to determine whether the person should be conditionally released or discharged.

161.346 *Hearings on discharge, conditional release, commitment or modification; psychiatric reports; notice of hearing; hearing rights.* (1) The board shall conduct a hearing upon any application for discharge, conditional release, commitment or modification filed pursuant to ORS 161.336 or 161.341:

(a) If the board finds that the person is no longer affected by mental disease or defect, or, if so affected, that he no longer presents a substantial danger to himself or others, the board shall order him discharged from commitment or from conditional release.

(b) If the board finds that the person is still affected by a mental disease or defect and is a substantial danger to himself or others, but can be controlled adequately if he is conditionally released with treatment as a condition of release, the board shall order him conditionally released as provided in ORS 161.336.

(c) If the board finds that the person has not recovered from his mental disease or defect and is a substantial danger to himself or others and cannot adequately be controlled if he is conditionally released on supervision, the board shall order him committed to or retained in a state hospital designated by the Mental Health Division for care, custody and treatment.

(2) In any hearing under this section, the board may appoint a psychiatrist or licensed psychologist to examine the person and to submit a report to the board. Reports filed with the board pursuant to the examination shall include, but need not be limited to, an opinion as to the mental condition of the person and whether the person presents a substantial danger to himself or others, and whether the person could be adequately controlled with treatment as a condition of release. To facilitate the examination of the person, the board may order the person placed in the temporary custody of any state hospital or other suitable facility.

(3) The board may make the determination regarding discharge or conditional release based upon the written reports submitted pursuant to this section. If any member of the board desires further information from the examining psychiatrist or licensed psychologist who submitted the report, these persons shall be summoned by the board to give testimony. The board shall consider all other evidence regarding the person's mental condition, including but not limited to the record of trial, the information supplied by the district attorney for the court or department of the county from which the person was committed or by any other interested party, including the person. A written record shall be kept of all proceedings before the board.

(4) The person about whom the hearing is being conducted shall be furnished with written notice of any hearing pending under this section within a reasonable time prior to the hearing. The notice shall include:

(a) The time, place and location of the hearing.

(b) The nature of the hearing and the specific action for which a hearing has been requested.

(c) A statement of the right to consult with legal counsel, and if indigent, to have legal counsel provided without cost.

(d) A statement of the right to examine, prior to the hearing, all relevant information, documents and reports in the board's possession.

(5) At the hearing, the person subject to the provision of ORS 137.540, 161.315 to 161.351, 161.385 to 161.395, 192.690 and 428.210 shall have the right:

(a) To appear at all proceedings held pursuant to this section, except board deliberations.

(b) To cross-examine all witnesses giving testimony at the hearing.

(c) To subpoena witnesses.

(d) To be represented by legal counsel and, if indigent, to have counsel provided without cost.

161.351 *Discharge of person under jurisdiction of Psychiatric Security Review Board; burden of proof; periodic review of status; notices; challenge of status determination.* (1) Any person placed under the jurisdiction of the Psychiatric Security Review Board pursuant to ORS 161.336 or 161.341, shall be discharged at such time as the board shall find by a preponderance of the evidence that the person is no longer affected by mental disease or defect, or, if he continues to be so affected, that he no longer presents a substantial danger to himself or others which requires regular medical care, medication, supervision or treatment.

(2) For purposes of this section, a person affected by a mental disease or defect in a state of remission is considered to have a mental disease or defect. A person whose mental disease or defect may, with reasonable medical probability, occasionally become active and when it becomes active will render him a danger to himself or others, shall not be discharged. The state has the burden of proving by a preponderance of the evidence that the person continues to be affected by mental disease or defect and he continues to be a substantial danger to himself or others. The person shall continue under such supervision and treatment as the board deems necessary to protect the person and others.

(3) Any person who has been placed under the jurisdiction of the board under an order of conditional release for a period of 10 years shall be brought before the board for hearing within 30 days of the expiration of the 10-year period. The board shall review the person's status and determine whether he should be discharged from the jurisdiction of the board.

(4) If the person has been committed to a state hospital designated by the Mental Health Division, the superintendent of the hospital shall notify the board and the committing court or department of the expiration of the 10-year period. The notice shall be given at least 30 days prior to the expiration of the 10-year period. After receiving the notice, the board shall order a hearing.

(5) The notice provided in subsection (4) of this section shall contain a recommendation by the superintendent of the hospital either:

(a) That the person is still affected by a mental disease or defect but is no longer a substantial danger to himself or others and should be discharged.

(b) That the person continues to be affected by a mental disease or defect and is a substantial danger to himself or others and should continue in commitment; or

(c) That the person is no longer affected by a mental disease or defect and should be discharged.

(6) If the recommendation of the superintendent of the hospital is that the person should continue under the jurisdiction of the board, the person seeking discharge has the burden at the hearing of proving by a preponderance of the evidence that he:

(a) Is no longer affected by a mental disease or defect; or

(b) If so affected, is no longer a substantial danger to himself or others.

(7) If the state wishes to challenge the recommendation of the superintendent of the hospital for discharge, the state has the burden of proving by a preponderance of the evidence that the person seeking release continues to be affected by a mental disease or defect and is a substantial danger to himself or others.

(8) If the recommendation of the superintendent of the hospital is that the person should continue in commitment, the superintendent shall notify in writing the board and the circuit court or department and district attorney of the county of the original commitment and request that commitment proceedings be instituted as provided in ORS Chapter 426.

161.360 *Mental disease or defect excluding fitness to proceed.* (1) If, before or during the trial in any criminal case, the court has reason to doubt the defendant's fitness to proceed by reason of incompetence, the court may order an examination in the manner provided in ORS 161.365.

(2) A defendant may be found incompetent if, as a result of mental disease or defect, he is unable:

(a) To understand the nature of the proceedings against him; or

(b) To assist and cooperate with his counsel; or

(c) To participate in his defense.

161.365 *Procedure for determining issue of fitness to proceed.* (1) Whenever the court has reason to doubt the defendant's fitness to proceed by reason of incompetence as defined in ORS 161.360, the court may call to its assistance in reaching its decision any witness and may appoint a psychiatrist to examine the defendant and advise the court.

(2) If the court determines the assistance of a psychiatrist would be helpful, the court may order the defendant to be committed to a state mental hospital designated by the Mental Health Division for the purpose of an examination for a period not exceeding 30 days. The report of examination shall include, but is not necessarily limited to, the following:

(a) A description of the nature of the examination;

(b) A statement of the mental condition of the defendant; and

(c) If the defendant suffers from a mental disease or defect, an opinion as to whether he is incompetent within the definition set out in ORS 161.360.

(3) Except where the defendant and the court both request to the contrary, the report shall not contain any findings or conclusions as to whether the defendant as a result of mental disease or defect was responsible for the criminal act charged.

If the examination by the psychiatrist cannot be conducted by reason of the unwillingness of the defendant to participate therein, the report shall so state and shall include, if possible, an opinion as to whether such unwillingness of the defendant was the result of mental disease or defect affecting his competency to proceed.

(5) The report of the examination shall be filed in triplicate with the clerk of the court, who shall cause copies to be delivered to the district attorney and to counsel for defendant.

(6) The court, when it has ordered a psychiatric examination, shall order the county wherein the original proceeding was commenced to pay:

(a) A reasonable fee if the examination of the defendant is conducted by a psychiatrist in private practice; and

(b) All costs including transportation of the defendant if the examination is conducted by a psychiatrist in the employ of the Mental Health Division or a community mental health program established under ORS 430.610 to 430.670.

161.370 *Determination of fitness; effect of finding of unfitness; proceedings if fitness regained; pretrial objections by defense counsel.* (1) When the defendant's fitness to proceed is drawn in question, the issue shall be determined by the court. If neither the prosecuting attorney nor counsel for the defendant contests the finding of the report filed by a psychiatrist under ORS 161.365, the court may make the determination on the basis of such report. If the finding is contested, the court shall hold a hearing on the issue. If the report is received in evidence upon such hearing, the party who contests the finding thereof shall have the right to summon and to cross-examine the psychiatrist or psychiatrists who submitted the report and to offer evidence upon the issue. Other evidence regarding the defendant's fitness to proceed may be introduced by either party.

(2) If the court determines that the defendant lacks fitness to proceed, the proceeding against him shall be suspended, except as provided in subsection (5) of this section, and the court shall commit him to the custody of the superintendent of a

state mental hospital designated by the Mental Health Division or shall release him on supervision for so long as such unfitness shall endure. The court may release the defendant on supervision if it determines that care other than commitment for incompetency to stand trial would better serve the defendant and the community. It may place conditions which it deems appropriate on the release, including the requirement that the defendant regularly report to the Mental Health Division or a community mental health program for examination to determine if the defendant has regained his competency to stand trial. When the court, on its own motion or upon the application of the superintendent of the hospital in which the defendant is committed, a person examining the defendant as a condition of his release on supervision, or either party, determines, after a hearing, if a hearing is requested, that the defendant has regained fitness to proceed, the proceeding shall be resumed. If, however, the court is of the view that so much time has elapsed since the commitment or release of the defendant on supervision that it would be unjust to resume the criminal proceeding, the court on motion of either party may dismiss the charge and may order the defendant to be discharged or cause a proceeding to be commenced forthwith under ORS 426.070 to 426.170.

(3) Notwithstanding subsection (2) of this section, a defendant who remains committed under this section to the custody of a state mental hospital designated by the Mental Health Division for a period of time equal to the maximum term of the sentence which could be imposed if the defendant were convicted of the offense with which he is charged or for five years, whichever is less, shall be discharged at the end of the period. The superintendent of the hospital in which the defendant is committed shall notify the committing court of the expiration of the period at least 30 days prior to the date of expiration. The notice shall include an opinion as to whether the defendant is still incompetent within the definition set forth in ORS 161.360. Upon receipt of the notice, the court shall dismiss the charge and shall order the defendant to be discharged or cause a proceeding to be commenced forthwith under ORS 426.070 to 426.170.

(4) If the defendant regains fitness to proceed, the term of any sentence received by the defendant for conviction of the crime charged shall be reduced by the amount of time the defendant was committed under this section to the custody of a state mental hospital designated by the Mental Health Division.

(5) The fact that the defendant is unfit to proceed does not preclude any objection through counsel and without the personal participation of the defendant on the grounds that the indictment is insufficient, that the statute of limitations has run, that double jeopardy principles apply or upon any other ground at the discretion of the court which the court deems susceptible of fair determination prior to trial.

161.380 *Incapacity due to immaturity.* (1) A person who is tried as an adult in a court of criminal jurisdiction is not criminally responsible for any conduct which occurred when the person was under 14 years of age.

(2) Incapacity due to immaturity, as defined in subsection (1) of this section, is a defense.

161.385 *Psychiatric Security Review Board; composition, term of office, qualifications, compensation, appointment and meetings; judicial review of board order.* (1) There is hereby created a Psychiatric Security Review Board consisting of five members appointed by the Governor and subject to confirmation by the Senate by the affirmative vote of a majority of the Senators voting, a quorum being present.

If an appointment is made when the Legislative Assembly is not in session, the Senate shall act through the Committee on Executive Appointments under ORS 171.560.

(2) The membership of the board shall be composed of:

(a) A psychiatric experienced in the criminal justice system and not otherwise employed on a full-time basis by the Mental Health Division or a community mental health program;

(b) A licensed psychologist experienced in the criminal justice system and not otherwise employed on a full-time basis by the Mental Health Division or a community mental health program;

(c) A member with substantial experience in the processes of parole and probation;

(c) A member of the general public; and

(e) A lawyer with substantial experience in criminal trial practice.

(3) The term of office of each member is four years. The Governor at any time may remove any member for inefficiency, neglect of duty or malfeasance in office. Before the expiration of the term of a member, the Governor shall appoint a successor whose term begins on July 1 next following. A member is eligible for reappointment. If there is a vacancy for any cause, the Governor shall make an appointment to become immediately effective for the unexpired term.

(4) Notwithstanding the term of office specified by subsection (3) of this section, of the members first appointed to the board:

(a) One shall serve for a term ending June 30, 1979.

(b) Two shall serve for terms ending June 30, 1980.

(c) Two shall serve for terms ending June 30, 1981.

(5) A member of the board not otherwise employed full time by the state, shall be paid on a per diem basis an amount equal to four percent of the gross monthly salary of a member of the State Board of Parole for each day during which the member is engaged in the performance of his official duties, including necessary travel time. In addition, subject to ORS 292.220 to 292.250 regulating travel and other expenses of state officers and employes, he shall be reimbursed for actual and necessary travel and other expenses incurred by him in the performance of his official duties.

(6) Subject to any applicable provision of the State Merit System Law, the board may hire employes to aid it in performing its duties under ORS 137.540, 161.315 to 161.351, 161.385 to 161.395, 192.690 and 428.210.

(7) (a) The board shall select one of its members as chairman to serve for a one-year term with such duties and powers as the board determines.

(b) A majority of the voting members of the board constitutes a quorum for the transaction of business.

(8) The board shall meet at least twice every month, unless the chairman determines that there is not sufficient business before the board to warrant a meeting at the scheduled time. The board shall also meet at other times and places specified by the call of the chairman or of a majority of the members of the board.

(9) (a) When a person over whom the board exercises its jurisdiction is adversely affected or aggrieved by a final order of the board, the person is entitled to judicial review of the final order. The person shall be entitled to counsel and, if indigent, counsel shall be provided.

(b) The order and the proceedings underlying the order are subject to review by the Court of Appeals upon petition to that court filed within 60 days of the order for which review is sought. The board shall submit to the court the record of the proceeding or, if the person agrees, a shortened record. A copy of the record transmitted shall be delivered to the person by the board.

(c) The court may affirm, reverse or remand the order on the same basis as provided in paragraphs (a) to (d) of subsection (8) of ORS 183.482.

(d) The filing of the petition shall not stay the board's order, but the board or the Court of Appeals may order a stay upon application on such terms as are deemed proper.

161.390 *Mental Health Division to promulgate rules for assignment of persons to state mental hospitals.* The Mental Health Division shall promulgate rules for the assignment of persons to state mental hospitals under ORS 161.351, 161.365 and 161.370 and for establishing standards for evaluation and treatment of persons committed to a state hospital designated by the division or ordered to a community mental health program under ORS 137.540, 161.315 to 161.351, 161.385 to 161.395, 192.690 and 428.210.

161.395 *Subpoena power of Psychiatric Security Review Board.* (1) Upon request of any party to a hearing before the board, the board or its designated representatives shall issue, or the board on its own motion may issue, subpoenas requiring the attendance and testimony of witnesses.

(2) Upon request of any party to the hearing before the board and upon a proper showing of the general relevance and reasonable scope of the documentary or physical evidence sought, the board or its designated representative shall issue, or the board on its own motion may issue, subpoenas duces tecum.

(3) Witnesses appearing under subpoenas, other than the parties or state officers or employes, shall receive fees and mileage as prescribed by law for witnesses in civil actions. If the board or its designated representative certifies that the testimony of a witness was relevant and material, any person who has paid fees and mileage to that witness shall be reimbursed by the board.

(4) If any person fails to comply with a subpoena issued under subsections (1) or (2) of this section or any party or witness refuses to testify regarding any matter on which he may be lawfully interrogated, the judge of the circuit court of any county, on the application of the board or its designated representative of or the party requesting the issuance of the subpoena, shall compel obedience by proceedings for contempt as in the case of disobedience of the requirements of a subpoena issued by the court.

(5) If any person, agency, or facility fails to comply with an order of the board issued pursuant to subsection (2) of this section, the judge of a circuit court of any county, on application of the board or its designated representative, shall compel obedience by proceedings for contempt as in the case of disobedience of the requirements of an order issued by the court. Contempt for disobedience of an order of the board shall be punishable by a fine of $100.

Appendix C: Sample Forms Regarding Mental Disease or Defect

SAMPLE FORM NUMBER 1

MOTION FOR PSYCHIATRIC EXAM

IN THE *DISTRICT/CIRCUIT COURT OF THE STATE OF OREGON FOR LANE COUNTY

Case No. *

THE STATE OF OREGON,	)	
	)	
Plaintiff,	)	
	)	
vs.	)	M O T I O N
	)	
*DEFENDANT'S NAME,	)	
	)	
Defendant.	)	

COMES NOW the State of Oregon by the District Attorney for Lane County and moves the court to enter an order herein directing the defendant, *DEFENDANT'S NAME, to present *HIMSELF/HERSELF at a time and place to be set by order of the court for the purpose of a Minnesota Multi-Phasic Personality Inventory test in order to aid *NAME OF DOCTOR in his psychiatric evaluation, and to present *HIMSELF/HERSELF at a time and place to be set by order of the court for the purpose of being psychiatrically examined by *NAME OF DOCTOR on behalf of the State of Oregon to determine whether or not at the time of crime charged in the indictment the defendant lacked substantial capacity either to appreciate the criminality of *HIS/HER conduct or to conform *HIS/HER conduct to the requirements of the law as a result of mental disease or defect as defined in ORS 161.295; and whether the defendant did or did not have the capacity to form the requisite intent which is an element of the crime charged in the indictment as a result of mental disease or defect as defined in ORS 161.300.

This motion is made pursuant to ORS 161.315 and is based upon the notice filed herein of defense counsel's intention to produce evidence that the defendant was not legally responsible for the facts alleged in the indictment because of mental or emotional defect, disease or condition.

Dated this *DATE.

*D.A.'S NAME, District Attorney

By_____

*DEPUTY D.A.'S NAME
Assistant District Attorney

SAMPLE FORM NUMBER 1A

MOTION FOR PSYCHIATRIC EXAM

IN THE *DISTRICT/CIRCUIT COURT OF THE STATE OF OREGON FOR LANE COUNTY

Case No. *

THE STATE OF OREGON,	)	
	)	
Plaintiff,	)	
	)	
vs.	)	M O T I O N
	)	
*DEFENDANT'S NAME,	)	
	)	
Defendant.	)	

COMES NOW the State of Oregon by the District Attorney for Lane County and moves the court to enter an order herein directing the defendant, *DEFENDANT'S NAME, to present *HIMSELF/HERSELF at a time and place to be set by order of the court for the purpose of being psychiatrically examined by a duly qualified psychiatrist on behalf of the State of Oregon to determine whether or not at the time of crime charged in the indictment, the defendant lacked substantial capacity either to appreciate the criminality of *HIS/HER conduct or to conform *HIS/HER conduct to the requirements of the law as a result of mental disease or defect as defined in ORS 161.295; and whether the defendant did or did not have the capacity to form the requisite intent which is an element of the crime charged in the indictment as a result of mental disease or defect as defined in ORS 161.300.

This motion is made pursuant to ORS 161.315 and is based upon the notice filed herein of defense counsel's intention to produce evidence that the defendant was not legally responsible for the facts alleged in the indictment because of mental or emotional defect, disease or condition.

Dated this *DATE.

*D.A.'S NAME, District Attorney

By_____
                *DEPUTY D.A.'S NAME
                Assistant District Attorney

SAMPLE FORM NUMBER 2

ORDER FOR PSYCHIATRIC EXAM

IN THE *DISTRICT/CIRCUIT COURT OF THE STATE OF OREGON FOR LANE COUNTY

Case No. *

THE STATE OF OREGON,	)	
	)	
Plaintiff,	)	
	)	
vs.	)	O R D E R
	)	
*DEFENDANT'S NAME,	)	
	)	
Defendant.	)	

THIS MATTER having come on before the court on the motion of the District Attorney for Lane County the State of Oregon, by *DEPUTY D.A.'S NAME, Assistant District Attorney, for an order directing the defendant, *DEFENDANT'S NAME, to present *HIMSELF/HERSELF at a designated time and place for the purpose of a Minnesota Multi-Phasic Personality Inventory test in order to aid *NAME OF DOCTOR in his psychiatric evaluation, and to present *HIMSELF/HERSELF at a designated time and place for the purpose of being psychiatrically examined on behalf of the State of Oregon to determine whether or not at the time of the crime charged in the indictment the defendant suffered from a disease, defect or condition of the mind which would be a legal defense to the crime charged in the indictment, and the court having examined the motion filed on behalf of the state, and having considered the authority of ORS 161.315; and

IT APPEARING TO THE COURT that the state is entitled to conduct a Minnesota Multi-Phasic Personality Inventory test and a psychiatric examination of the defendant,

*   OPTIONAL PARAGRAPHS:

NOW, THEREFORE, IT IS HEREBY ORDERED that *DEFENDANT'S NAME present *HIMSELF/HERSELF at the office of *NAME OF DOCTOR AND ADDRESS at *TIME for the purpose of a Minnesota Multi-Phasic Personality Inventory test in order to aid *NAME OF DOCTOR in his evaluation of the said defendant; and

OR:

NOW, THEREFORE, IT IS HEREBY ORDERED that a Minnesota Multi-Phasic Personality Inventory test be conducted at the Lane County Jail at a time convenient to *NAME OF PERSON ADMINISTERING TEST and the Lane County Jail for the purpose of aiding *NAME OF DOCTOR in his evaluation of the said defendant; and

SAMPLE FORM NUMBER 2 - Cont.

IT IS FURTHER ORDERED that *THE LANE COUNTY SHERIFF TRANSPORT THE DEFENDANT, * DEFENDANT'S NAME, TO BE PERSONALLY PRESENT AT the office of *NAME OF DOCTOR AND ADDRESS at *TIME for the purpose of there being psychiatrically examined by *NAME OF DOCTOR to determine whether or not at the time of the crime charged in the indictment the defendant lacked substantial capacity either to appreciate the criminality of *HIS/HER conduct or to conform *HIS/HER conduct to the requirements of law as a result of mental disease or defect as defined in ORS 161.295; and whether the defendant did or did not have the capacity in the indictment as a result of mental disease or defect as defined in ORS 161.300.

IT IS FURTHER ORDERED that *NAME OF ATTORNEY, attorney for defendant, may be present at said examination; and

IT IS FURTHER ORDERED that *NAME OF DOCTOR submit a written report of the results of his examination to the District Attorney for Lane County.

Dated this *DATE.

_____
*DISTRICT/CIRCUIT COURT JUDGE

SAMPLE FORM NUMBER 2A

ORDER FOR PSYCHIATRIC EXAM

IN THE *DISTRICT/CIRCUIT COURT OF THE STATE OF OREGON FOR LANE COUNTY

Case No. *

```
THE STATE OF OREGON,         )
                             )
                Plaintiff,   )
                             )
       vs.                   )              O R D E R
                             )
*DEFENDANT'S NAME,           )
                             )
              Defendant.     )
```

THIS MATTER having come before the court on the motion of the District Attorney for Lane County the State of Oregon, by *DEPUTY D.A.'S NAME, Assistant District Attorney, for an order directing the defendant, *DEFENDANT'S NAME, to present *HIMSELF/HERSELF at a designated time and place for the purpose of being psychiatrically examined on behalf of the State of Oregon to determine whether or not at the time of the crime charged in the indictment the defendant suffered from a disease, defect or condition of the mind which would be a legal defense to the crime charged in the indictment, and the court having examined the motion filed on behalf of the state, and having considered the authority of ORS 161.315; and

IT APPEARING TO THE COURT that the state is entitled to conduct a psychiatric examination of the defendant,

NOW, THEREFORE, IT IS HEREBY ORDERED that *DEFENDANT'S NAME present *HIMSELF/HERSELF at LOCATION AND TIME for the purpose of being psychiatrically examined by *NAME OF DOCTOR, to determine whether or not at the time of the crime charged in the indictment the defendant lacked substantial capacity either to appreciate the criminality of *HIS/HER conduct or to conform *HIS/HER conduct to the requirements of law as a result of mental disease or defect as defined in ORS 161.295; and whether the defendant did or did not have the capacity to form the requisite intent which is an element of the crime charged in the indictment as a result of mental disease or defect as defined in ORS 161.300.

IT IS FURTHER ORDERED that *NAME OF ATTORNEY, attorney for defendant, may be present at said examination; and

IT IS FURTHER ORDERED that the said *NAME OF DOCTOR submit a written report of the results of his examination to the District Attorney for Lane County.

Dated this *DATE.

_____
*DISTRICT/CIRCUIT COURT JUDGE

SAMPLE FORM NUMBER 3

MOTION FOR PSYCHOLOGICAL TESTING

IN THE *DISTRICT/CIRCUIT COURT OF THE STATE OF OREGON FOR LANE COUNTY

Case No. *

THE STATE OF OREGON,	)	
	)	
Plaintiff,	)	
	)	
vs.	)	M O T I O N
	)	
*DEFENDANT'S NAME,	)	
	)	
Defendant.	)	

COMES NOW the State of Oregon by the District Attorney for Lane County and moves the court for an order directing the defendant, DEFEN-DANT'S NAME, to present *HIMSELF/HERSELF at a time and place to be set by order of the court for the purpose of being psychologically tested by a duly qualified psychologist pursuant to the direction of the examining psychiatrist. This motion is based upon the request of the examining psychiatrist to assist him in rendering an opinion pursuant to the order of the court dated the *DATE OF ORDER FOR PSYCHIATRIC EXAM.

Dated this *DATE.

*D.A.'S NAME, District Attorney

By_____
   *DEPUTY D.A.'S NAME
   Assistant District Attorney

SAMPLE FORM NUMBER 4

ORDER FOR PSYCHOLOGICAL TESTING

IN THE *DISTRICT/CIRCUIT COURT OF THE STATE OF OREGON FOR LANE COUNTY

Case No. *

THE STATE OF OREGON,	)	
	)	
Plaintiff,	)	
	)	
vs.	)	O R D E R
	)	
*DEFENDANT'S NAME,	)	
	)	
Defendant.	)	

    THIS MATTER having come before the court on the motion of the State of Oregon by the Lane County District Attorney for an order directing the defendant to present *HIMSELF/HERSELF at a designated time and place for the purpose of being psychologically examined and tested by request of the examining psychiatrist pursuant to the order of the court entered herein on the *DATE OF ORDER FOR PSYCHIATRIC EXAM; and

    IT APPEARING TO THE COURT that the State is entitled to have the defendant psychologically examined and tested,

    NOW, THEREFORE, IT IS HEREBY ORDERED that the defendant, *DEFEN-DANT'S NAME, BE PERSONALLY PRESENT AT THE OFFICE OF *NAME OF DOCTOR AND ADDRESS, AT *TIME ON *DATE for the purpose of being psychologically examined and tested for the purpose of aiding *NAME OF DOCTOR in rendering an opinion as to whether or not at the time of the crime charged in the indictment the defendant lacked substantial capacity either to appreciate the criminality of *HIS/HER conduct or to conform *HIS/HER conduct to the requirements of law as a result of mental disease or defect as defined in ORS 161.295; and whether the defendant did or did not have the capacity in the indictment as a result of mental disease or defect as defined in ORS 161.300.

    Dated this *DATE.

_____
    *DISTRICT/CIRCUIT COURT JUDGE

SAMPLE FORM NUMBER 5

MOTION FOR ORDER TO PRODUCE PRISONER

IN THE *DISTRICT/CIRCUIT COURT OF THE STATE OF OREGON FOR LANE COUNTY

Case No. *

THE STATE OF OREGON,	)	
	)	
Plaintiff,	)	
	)	
vs.	)	M O T I O N
	)	
*DEFENDANT'S NAME,	)	
	)	
Defendant.	)	

COMES NOW *D.A.'S NAME, District Attorney for Lane County, and moves the court for an order directing the Sheriff of Lane County to return the defendant, *DEFENDANT'S NAME, from the Oregon State Hospital, Salem, Oregon to appear before this court for further proceedings herein.

In support of this motion, it is represented to the court that the prosecution has received information from competent authority at the Oregon State Hospital, Salem, Oregon to the effect that the defendant's mental condition is such that he may now appear further in connection with the above-entitled matter.

Dated this *DATE.

*D.A.'S NAME, District Attorney

By_____
            *DEPUTY D.A.'S NAME
            Assistant District Attorney

SAMPLE FORM NUMBER 6

ORDER TO PRODUCE PRISONER FOR FITNESS HEARING

IN THE *DISTRICT/CIRCUIT COURT OF THE STATE OF OREGON FOR LANE COUNTY

Case No. *

THE STATE OF OREGON,   )
)
                    Plaintiff,   )
)
          vs.   )   O R D E R
)
*DEFENDANT'S NAME,   )
)
                    Defendant.   )

     THIS MATTER having come on before the court on the motion of *D.A.'S
NAME, District Attorney for Lane County, for an order directing the
return of the defendant to appear further before this court, and

     IT APPEARING to the court that the mental condition of the defen-
dant, *DEFENDANT'S NAME, is now such that he should be returned before
this court for further proceedings in connection with the above-entitled
matter and the court being fully advised,

     NOW, THEREFORE, IT IS HEREBY ORDERED that the Sheriff of Lane
County transport the defendant, *DEFENDANT'S NAME, from the Oregon State
Hospital, Salem, Oregon to appear before this court on the *DATE AND
TIME for further proceedings herein.

     Dated this *DATE.

                                  _____
                                  *DISTRICT/CIRCUIT COURT JUDGE

SAMPLE FORM NUMBER 7

ORDER DENYING MENTAL DISEASE AND ORDER TO PROCEED

IN THE *DISTRICT/CIRCUIT COURT OF THE STATE OF OREGON FOR LANE COUNTY

Case No. *

```
THE STATE OF OREGON,              )
                                  )
                 Plaintiff,       )
                                  )
        vs.                       )          O R D E R
                                  )
*DEFENDANT'S NAME,                )
                                  )
                 Defendant.       )
```

THIS MATTER having come on before the court for hearing on the *DATE OF HEARING, the State of Oregon appearing by and through *DEPUTY D.A.'S NAME, Assistant District Attorney for Lane County, and the defendant, *DEFENDANT'S NAME, appearing personally and by and through his attorney, *NAME OF DEFENSE COUNSEL, and this being the time set for hearing to determine whether or not the defendant is suffering from a mental disease or defect rendering him unable to understand the nature of the proceedings against him or unable to assist and participate in his defense, and the court having heard the testimony of *NAME OF PYCHIATRIST, a duly qualified psychiatrist, the testimony of *NAME OF WITNESS, a lay witness, having reviewed the written report of *NAME OF PSYCHIATRIST, a duly qualified psychiatrist, and having considered statements of counsel; and the court being fully advised;

IT IS THE FINDING of this court that the defendant, *DEFENDANT'S NAME, is not suffering from a mental disease or defect to an extent rendering him unable to understand the nature of the proceedings against him or unable to assist and participate in his defense and that this matter should proceed accordingly.

NOW, THEREFORE, IT IS HEREBY ORDERED that this matter proceed for entry of plea at *DATE OF ARRAIGNMENT.

Dated this *DATE.

_____
*DISTRICT/CIRCUIT COURT JUDGE

SAMPLE FORM NUMBER 8

ORDER COMMITTING DEFENDANT TO OREGON STATE HOSPITAL

IN THE *DISTRICT/CIRCUIT COURT OF THE STATE OF OREGON FOR LANE COUNTY

Case No. *

THE STATE OF OREGON,	)	
	)	
Plaintiff,	)	
	)	
vs.	)	O R D E R
	)	
*DEFENDANT'S NAME,	)	
	)	
Defendant.	)	

THIS MATTER having come before the court for determination of defendant's fitness to proceed by reason of incompetence as defined in ORS 161.360, the defendant being personally present and represented by his attorney, *NAME OF DEFENSE COUNSEL, and the State being represented by *DEPUTY D.A.'S NAME, Assistant District Attorney, and the court having considered written psychiatric reports and having heard testimony, and finding defendant to be unfit to proceed by reason of incompetence and being otherwise fully advised in the premises; now, therefore,

IT IS HEREBY ORDERED that the defendant, *DEFENDANT'S NAHE, be and *HE/SHE hereby is committed to the legal and physical custody of the Superintendent of the Oregon State Hospital for so long as such unfitness shall endure.

IT IS FURTHER ORDERED that the Lane County Sheriff transport the defendant to the Oregon State Hospital forthwith.

Dated this *DATE.

_____
*DISTRICT/CIRCUIT COURT JUDGE

SAMPLE FORM NUMBER 9

ORDER, VERDICT OF COURT, AND JUDGMENT OF ACQUITTAL

IN THE *DISTRICT/CIRCUIT COURT OF THE STATE OF OREGON FOR LANE COUNTY

Case No. *

THE STATE OF OREGON,	)	
	)	
Plaintiff,	)	
	)	
vs.	)	ORDER, VERDICT OF COURT AND
	)	JUDGMENT OF ACQUITTAL
*DEFENDANT'S NAME,	)	
	)	
Defendant.	)	

   THIS MATTER having come before the court upon the stipulation of
the parties as to the testimony of witnesses including the reports of
psychiatrists and a psychologist, the State of Oregon appearing by
*DEPUTY D.A.'S NAME, Assistant District Attorney for Lane County, and
the defendant appearing personally and by and through his attorney,
*NAME OF DEFENSE COUNSEL, and the court having heard the stipulation of
parties, and now being fully advised;

   NOW THEREFORE, IT IS THE FINDING OF THE COURT that the defendant,
*DEFENDANT'S NAME, committed the acts charged in *INDICTMENT NO./COM-
PLAINT NO./INFORMATION NO./CITATION NO..

   IT IS THE FURTHER FINDING OF THE COURT that the defendant, *DEFEN-
DANT'S NAME, at the time of the commission of the acts set forth in
*INDICTMENT NO./COMPLAINT NO./INFORMATION NO./CITATION NO. was not
responsible for his criminal conduct because he was suffering from
mental disease or defect and lacked substantial capacity to appreciate
the criminality of his conduct or to conform his conduct to the requirements of law and lacked the capacity to form the intent required in
*INDICTMENT NO./COMPLAINT NO./INFORMATION NO./CITATION NO.

   IT IS THE FURTHER FINDING OF THE COURT that the defendant is still
affected by mental disease and defect and that he presents a substantial
danger to himself or the person of others and that he is in need of
care, supervision and treatment.

   NOW, THEREFORE, IT IS VERDICT OF THE COURT that the defendant is
not responsible for the crime charged in *INDICTMENT NO./COMPLAINT NO./
INFORMATION NO./CITATION NO. by reason of mental disease or defect
excluding criminal responsibility.

SAMPLE FORM NUMBER 9 - Cont.

NOW, THEREFORE, IT IS THE ORDER OF THE COURT that the defendant be placed under the jurisdiction of the Psychiatric Security Review Board for care and treatment, and the defendant is hereby remanded to the custody of the Mental Health Division of the State of Oregon to be henceforth transported by the Lane County Sheriff's Office to the Oregon State Hospital pending the defendant's hearing before the Psychiatric Security Review Board as provided by statute.

Dated this *DATE.

_____

*DISTRICT/CIRCUIT COURT JUDGE

SAMPLE FORM NUMBER 10

ORDER COMMITTING DEFENDANT TO OREGON STATE HOSPITAL
UPON STIPULATION OF THE PARTIES

IN THE *DISTRICT/CIRCUIT COURT OF THE STATE OF OREGON FOR LANE COUNTY

Case No. *

THE STATE OF OREGON,	)	
	)	
Plaintiff,	)	
	)	
vs.	)	ORDER
	)	
*DEFENDANT'S NAME,	)	
	)	
Defendant.	)	

THIS MATTER having come before the court upon the stipulation of
the parties as to the testimony of witnesses including the reports of
psychiatrists and a psychologist, the State of Oregon appearing by
*DEPUTY D.A.'S NAME, Assistant District Attorney for Lane County, and
the defendant apppearing personally and by and through his attorney,
*NAME OF DEFENSE COUNSEL, and the court having heard the stipulation of
parties and now being fully advised;

NOW THERFORE, IT IS THE FINDING OF THE COURT that the defendant,
*DEFENDANT'S NAME, is affected by a mental disease and defect and is
unable to understand the nature of the proceedings against him, to
assist and cooperate with his counsel, and to participate in his defense.

NOW, THEREFORE, IT IS HEREBY ORDERED that all criminal proceedings
now pending in this court against the defendant be suspended until the
defendant regains his fitness to proceed;

IT IS THE FURTHER ORDER OF THE COURT that the defendant is hereby
remanded to the custody of the Mental Health Division of the State of
Oregon to be forthwith transported by the Lane County Sheriff's Office
to the Superintendent of the Oregon State Hospital at Salem, Oregon for
care and treatment pursuant to this order of the court and that the
defendant be maintained in the custody of the Oregon State Hospital
until such time as he regains his ability to proceed.

Dated this *DATE.

_____
*DISTRICT/CIRCUIT COURT JUDGE

Appendix D: American Psychological Association Amicus Brief

IN THE SUPREME COURT OF THE STATE OF CALIFORNIA

VITALY TARASOFF, et al.,

    Plaintiff and Appellant,

    vs.

THE REGENTS OF THE
UNIVERSITY OF
CALIFORNIA, et al.,

    Defendants and Respondents.

S.F. No. 23042
Super. Ct. No. 405694

BRIEF OF AMICI CURIAE
IN SUPPORT OF PETITION
FOR REHEARING

I. Interest of Amici Curiae

The American Psychiatric Association, founded in 1844, is the nation's largest organization of qualified doctors of medicine who specialize in psychiatry. Approximately 20,000 of the nation's 25,000 psychiatrists are members of the Association.

Area VI of the Assembly of the American Psychiatric Association is the constitutent organization representing all California members of the American Psychiatric Association. Area VI includes all California district branches of the American Psychiatric Association, including the Northern California Psychiatric Society. It has approximately 3,000 members.

The Northern California Psychiatric Society's jurisdiction includes that portion of California north of San Luis Obispo, with the exception of the Central Valley. Like its parent organization, the Northern California Psychiatric Society is an organization of qualified doctors of medicine who specialize in the practice of psychiatry.

The California State Psychological Association is an organization of California psychologists, the majority of whom are directly involved in psychotherapy. It is a state-wide affiliate of the American Psychological Association.

The San Francisco Psychoanalytic Institute and Society is an affiliate society of the American Psychoanalytic Association. It is the official representative of psychoanalysts in the Northern California area.

The California Society for Clinic Social Work is a state affiliate representing approximately 800 clinical social workers licensed to practice psychotherapy in this state.

The National Association of Social Workers Golden Gate Chapter is the professional organization representing 60,000 social workers nationwide, of whom 1,700 are members of the Golden Gate Chapter, whose jurisdiction comprises Alameda, Contra Costa, Marin, Napa, San Francisco and Solano Counties.

The California Hospital Association is a state-wide association of public and private hospitals, representing approximately 600 institutions. Many of these hospitals provide psychiatric services and care and provide facilities for treatment by private psychotherapists.

Each of these organizations has a professional commitment to the diagnosis, care and treatment of persons with mental or emotional problems. Each of these organizations is devoted to the maintenance of the highest standards of psychotherapeutic treatment and to the scrupulous adherence to codes of professional ethics applicable to the psychotherapeutic relationship. Recognizing that their high professional callings impose on them extraordinary responsibilities to their patients and society, the amicus organizations and their members are committed to fulfilling those obligations according to the highest prevailing standards of knowledge and skill.

Applicable professional ethics require that psychotherapists keep in strictest confidence revelations made to them by patients seeking help, and prohibit the therapist from doing anything in the course of diagnosis or treatment which might injure the best interests of the patient. Amici are convinced that strictest confidentiality is fundamental to the therapist-patient relationship so that troubled persons may feel free to seek professional help, cooperate fully in treatment, and as a result achieve the benefits of therapy.

Each of the amicus organizations is also committed to the principle that all persons with mental or emotional problems are entitled to receive the highest caliber of psychotherapeutic treatment. Amici are convinced that the duty to warn threatened victims enunciated in this Court's opinion will place a serious constraint upon the practice of psychotherapy, and consequently deny a substantial number of disturbed persons the requisite standard of treatment which is not only their need, but their right.

Amici are gravely concerned that the Court's natural sympathy for plaintiffs' misfortune in this most peculiar case should not lead to the enunciation of legal doctrines which will constrain and hinder the proper practice of psychotherapy. The background information on the realities of psychotherapeutic practice which this amicus brief attempts to provide demonstrates that under the impulse of the unfortunate and peculiar facts of this case, the Court has adopted a standard of conduct which is incapable of practical application in the psychotherapeutic relationship. In so doing the Court has upset the proper balance between the conditions necessary for the effective practice of psychotherapy and the requirements of public safety. For these reasons amici curiae urge that the Court grant the Petition for Rehearing, and reconsider the opinion previously rendered in this case in the light of the new information provided herein.

II. The Enunciated Duty to Warn Establishes an Unworkable Standard

The decision in this case holds that "a psychotherapist treating a mentally ill patient . . . bears the duty to use reasonable care to give threatened persons such warnings as are essential to avert foreseeable danger arising from his patient's condition or treatment" (Opinion, 15). This newly established duty to warn imposes an impossible burden upon the practice of psychotherapy. It requires the psychotherapist to perform a function which study after study has shown he is ill-equipped to undertake; namely, the prediction of his patient's potential dangerousness.

Additional problems in the practical application of the duty to warn will arise from its very amorphous formulation in the present opinion. Unaddressed are the problems of whom to warn when no specific victim is threatened, the degree of specificity required in the warning, the type of warning which must be given to those who already know at least to some extent that they are threatened, and so forth.

Nor is the only problem with the standard and its failure to define more precisely the warning which must be given. The duty to warn will require psychotherapists to reach premature judgments distinguishing between the patient's thoughts, feelings and impulses and his intention, if any, to act upon them. Furthermore, the very foundation of the test upon what a "reasonable psychotherapist" would do, conflicts with the fundamentally individuated nature of the psychotherapeutic relationship which joins the patient and psychotherapist in a cooperative venture unlike any other.

Finally, the duty to warn imposed by this court places psychotherapists on the horns of an impossible dilemma. Under the new rule, if a psychotherapist fails to warn a third person of threats made to him by the patient, the therapist opens himself to liability imposed in the clear 20/20 vision of hindsight. On the other hand, if the psychotherapist does warn the third person, and it is later deemed that the warning was unnecessary, he subjects himself to liability for wrongful invasion of his patient's right of privacy. Given the inherent unpredictability of violent tendencies, the choice left therapists by this court's decision is truly Hobbesonian.

A. *Psychotherapists Cannot Predict Violence*

The Court's formulation of the duty to warn fundamentally misconceives the skills of the psychotherapist in its assumption that mental health professionals are in some way more qualified than the general public to predict future violent behavior of their patients. Unfortunately, study after study has shown that this fond hope of the capability accurately to predict violence in advance is simply not fulfilled. The burden of his new duty to warn, therefore, is formulated and imposed without reference to the actual ability of the therapist to sustain it.

As the very recent American Psychiatric Association Task Force on Clinical Aspects of the Violent Individual reported:

> Neither psychiatrists nor anyone else have reliably demonstrated an ability to predict future violence or "dangerousness." Neither has any special psychiatric "expertise" in this area been established (American Psychiatric Association Task Force Report 8, *Clinical Aspects of the Violent Individual* (July, 1974), 28.)

To the same effect, it was recently stated:

> [B]ecause some ex-patients are involved in murders, rapes and other violent crimes, we call upon psychiatrists to predict which ones will become violent. Unfortunately, the *assumption that psychiatrists can accurately predict such behavior . . . lacks any empirical support*. Rappeport presents the problem: "There are no articles that would assist us to any great extent in determining who might be dangerous, particularly before he commits an offense." Seymour L. Halleck adds: "Research in the area of dangerous behavior . . . is practically nonexistent. Prediction studies which have examined the probability recidivism have not focused on the issue of dangerousness. If the psychiatrist or any other behavioral scientist were asked to show proof of his predictive skills, objective data could not be offered." (Steadman & Cocozza, *Stimulus/Response: We Can't Predict Who Is Dangerous*, 8 Psychology Today 32, 35 (January, 1975); emphasis added).

Other recent research reinforces the conclusion that therapists have no special expertise in the prognosis of violence. From an in-depth study of 256 cases of incompetent, indicted felony defendants for whom psychiatric determinations of dangerousness were necessitated by New York law, H.J. Steadman concluded:

> A question that might be raised at this point is whether our data can address the issue of the abilities of psychiatrists to make these predictions as to dangerousness. This question rests on the assumption that there are bases in psychiatric training, perspective, and skills that give psychiatrists a special ability to make such predictions. In the 256 cases studied here we

have examined how the psychiatric prediction of dangerous is actually being done. . . . There seemed to be little in the way of special abilities evident in these cases. It is our opinion that *our data*, together with a lack of documentation in the literature for psychiatric abilities to accurately predict dangerousness, *seriously question any assumption that there is such a special psychiatric expertise.* (Steadman, *Some Evidence on the Inadequacy of the Concept and Determination of Dangerousness in Law and Psychology*, 1 Journal of Psychiatry and Law 409, 421-2 (1973); emphasis added).

What these studies and numerous similar ones show is that absent a prior history of violence, no therapist can accurately predict whether his patient is in fact dangerous or not. This Court's newly formulated duty to warn directly conflicts with this growing body of scientific evidence. In the first place, it assumes that a "reasonable" psychotherapist will under certain circumstances be able to predict violence. In fact, the above-cited studies show that the reasonable therapist acting in conformity with the present standards of his profession cannot make any reliable prediction as to the possibility of his patients' future violence in the absence of a history of prior violent behavior.

The newly imposed duty to warn is also inconsistent with the finding of scientific research that no special professional ability or expertise has yet been demonstrated in the prognosis of dangerousness. Instead, the few studies which have been done "strongly suggest that psychiatrists are rather inaccurate predictors; inaccurate in an absolute sense, and even less accurate when compared with other professionals . . . and when compared to actuarial devices, such as prediction or experience tables." (Dershowitz, *the Law of Dangerousness*, 23 J. Legal Ed. 24, 46 (1970)) The California Legislature and the professions involved have recognized this problem by the passage of the Lanterman-Petris-Short Act (Welf. * Inst. Code, § 5000, *et seq.*), which greatly restricts the authority of psychotherapists to commit patients to mental institutions (see p. 42-43, *infra*).

Thus, the "special relationship" between the psychotherapist and his patient cannot be seen as giving rise to a duty to warn a threatened person since there is nothing "special" in that relationship which gives rise to an ability to predict violence. Indeed, if the Court is intent upon finding a duty to warn of potential aggressive acts, that duty should more properly attach to members of professions such as correctional officers, actuaries or members of the general public who have proven more able to make such predictions.

Appendix E:
United States v.
Beachley L. Wright

Notice: This opinion is subject to formal revision before publication in the Federal Reporter or U.S.App.D.C. Reports. Users are requested to notify the Clerk of any formal errors in order that corrections may be made before the bound volumes go to press.

United States Court of Appeals

FOR THE DISTRICT OF COLUMBIA CIRCUIT

No. 79-1124

UNITED STATES OF AMERICA

v.

BEACHEY L. WRIGHT, APPELLANT

Appeal from the United States District Court
for the District of Columbia

(D.C. Criminal 78-309-1)

Argued February 14, 1980

Decided April 22, 1980

Amy G. Budnick * with whom *Michael Zeldin* (Appointed by this Court) and *Sandra Richardson* * were on the brief, for appellant.

---

* Student Counsel.

William J. Bowman, Assistant United States Attorney
with whom *Carl S. Rauh*, United States Attorney (at the
time the brief was filed) *John A. Terry, Michael W. Far-
rell, Roger M. Adelman* and *John H. E. Bayly, Jr.*, Assistant United States Attorneys were on the brief, for
appellee.

Before BAZELON, *Senior Circuit Judge*, WILKEY and
WALD, *Circuit Judges*.

Opinion for the Court filed by *Senior Circuit Judge*
BAZELON.

Circuit Judge WILKEY concurs in the result and in
Parts I and II.

BAZELON, *Senior Circuit Judge*: After a two-day evidentiary hearing, the trial judge declined to interpose a
defense of insanity over the objections of appellant,
Beachey Wright. Wright was charged with destruction
of government property (18 U.S.C. § 1361). The indictment alleged that Wright damaged a model of the United
States Capitol building and its glass display case, both
housed in the Capitol.

Wright was convicted and sentenced to three years
imprisonment with credit for time served.[1] In this appeal, he contends that the trial judge abused his discretion in failing to raise the insanity defense *sua sponte*
over appellant's objections.

I.

A. *Events of May 16, 1978*

The facts are undisputed. Between 11:30 and 11:45 a.m.
on the day of the offense, appellant entered the United
States Capitol building, and began "walking around ob-

---

[1] The court ultimately reduced the sentence to time served
after Wright had spent 11 months in prison.

serving the tourists, taking in the building and the art-
works and exhibits that were on display." [2] Wright then
was "inspired" by the Holy Spirit to commit a symbolic
act, intended to warn people of God's impending judgment that the nation "has deviated from his original
designs."[3] Wright saw a metal stanchion, used with a
cordon to rope off displays. He also noticed a replica of
the Capitol building behind a glass display case. He
"tossed" the stanchion at the model and the glass case,
causing both to break.[4] A police officer on duty heard the
crash and arrested Wright.

B. *Mental Examinations and the Competency to Stand
    Trial Determination*

Following his arrest, appellant was committed to St.
Elizabeths Hospital for a mental examination pursuant
to 24 D.C.Code § 301 (a). The Hospital report represented the shared opinions of psychiatrist Dr. Glen H.
Miller, two other psychiatrists, a psychologist, and a social
worker. The report concluded that Wright was competent to stand trial, but had suffered from a mental
disease at the time of the offense; the report also diagnosed him as "Schizophrenia, paranoid type." [5]

---

[2] Trial Transcript, Dec. 6, 1978 (T.Tr.) at 102 (testimony
of Beachey Wright).

[3] *Id*. at 103-04 (testimony of Beachey Wright).

[4] *Id*. at 105 (testimony of Beachey Wright).

[5] [Wright] is competent for trial by virtue of having a
rational as well as a factual understanding of the proceedings pending against him and being able to consult
with counsel with a reasonable degree of rational understanding. Furthermore, on or about May 16, 1978, the
date of the alleged offense, he was suffering from a
mental disease which substantially impaired his behavioral controls, and the alleged offense, if committed by
him, was the product of mental disease. Although he knew

The judge found appellant competent to stand trial, but in light of the diagnosis, he ordered further psychiatric examination.[6] Informed by Wright's counsel that Wright would not rely on an insanity defense, the court also appointed an amicus curiae to advise the court whether it should impose the defense over Wright's objection. Amicus counsel recommended that an evidentiary hearing be held (1) to determine whether the court should *sua sponte* raise the insanity defense[7] and (2) to "explore carefully the quality of the defendant's decision not to raise the defense."[8]

C. *The Hearing*

Three psychiatrists testified at the two-day evidentiary hearing. All three testified that appellant was competent to stand trial,[9] but their diagnoses differed. Dr.

---

essentially the wrongfulness of his conduct, his mental disease prevented him from conforming his conduct to the requirements of the law.

Letter to Clerk, United States District Court for the District of Columbia, from Harold M. Boslow, Acting Chief, Pre-Trial Branch Division of Forensive Programs, St. Elizabeths Hospital.

[6] The court ordered further examination by the psychiatric staff of the District of Columbia Department of Human Resources, Forensic Psychiatric Services. The court also granted the government's motion to allow Dr. F. Jay Pepper to examine appellant.

[7] Memorandum of Amicus Curia (Oct. 2, 1978) at 13 [hereinafter cited as Amicus Memo #1].

[8] *Id.* (emphasis omitted).

[9] Dr. Glenn H. Miller found Wright competent to stand trial because "[h]e could have easily described to me all the roles of the people in the courtroom"; "he can [assist counsel] very ably"; and "he appreciated the wrongfulness of the act." Hearing Transcript, Oct. 11, 1978 (H.Tr.II) at 21-22. Dr. F. Jay Pepper said that the appellant demonstrated "that he

Miller, who contributed to the initial report by St. Elizabeths,[10] diagnosed Wright as suffering from schizophrenia,
paranoid type, at the time of the offense. He based his
conclusion on 1) appellant's conception of himself as
"God's harbinger for future destruction of the world"; [11]
2) his inability "to distinguish reality from fantasy in
important ways"; [12] and 3) his apparently compulsive
belief in his mission.[13] Dr. Miller concluded that the
appellant could "appreciate the wrongfulness of his act"
but "could not conform his conduct to the requirements
of law." [14] In addition, Dr. Miller saia appellant's decision not to raise the insanity defense was "tied in with
the psychosis," but not itself delusional.[15]

---

has a full understanding of what the whole process is about,
what pleas are open to him, what the consequences of those
pleas could be, what the maximum punishment is, and so
forth." Hearing Transcript, Oct. 10, 1978 (H.Tr.I) at 113.
Dr. Lawrence Sack concluded that Wright "has a rational
and factual understanding of the charges against him, able
to assist counsel, understands if convicted he bears the consequences for his actions." H.Tr.I at 71.

[10] The amicus counsel advised the court that "[i]n terms of
actual time spent with the defendant and materials reviewed,
Dr. Miller's examination appears to be the most thorough of
the three experts." Memorandum by Amicus Curiae (Oct. 20,
1978) at 4 n.2 [hereinafter cited as Amicus Memo #2].

[11] H.Tr.II at 10.

[12] *Id.* at 20.

[13] *See id.*

[14] *Id.* at 9.

[15] *Id.* at 14, 41. Dr. Miller said that Wright had "both rational and irrational reasons" for refusing to raise the defense.
Id. at 14. Dr. Miller reported that Wright understood the
difficulties in raising the defense, and also sought to avoid
"a very deep humiliation": he "would rather go around with
the label of 'criminal' than 'mentally ill'." *Id.* at 13. But the
decisive reasons, Dr. Miller recounted, were that Wright did

The two other psychiatrists testified that the appellant
was not psychotic at the time of the offense, although
there were paranoid elements to his thinking. Dr. Pepper
said that the appellant "likened himself to Old Testament
prophets and mentioned how they had been persecuted[,]
and I thought that this was a pretty good display of both
the grandiose and the persecutory aspects of the paranoid
thinking." [16] Nonetheless, Dr. Pepper testified that Wright
was able to distinguish what he thought was God's law
from human law, and was capable of choosing which to
obey.[17] Dr. Sack similarly found Wright to have "very
intense private religious beliefs" [18] and "paranoid thinking," but able to distinguish right from wrong.[19] Both
psychiatrists reported that Wright chose to avoid harm-
ing himself or the efficacy of his message when he declined
to raise the insanity defense.[20]

All three psychiatrists acknowledged that the appellant's case was a difficult one, and that he suffered from

---

not believe himself to be insane, and "he would actually be
willing to suffer, as I understand it, any amount of torment,
any amount of incarceration, any amount of humiliation to
bring forth his important view on God, and religion and the
world." *Id.* at 13-14. *See also id.* at 38. At the same time, Dr.
Miller concluded that Wright "is not delusionally avoiding
raising the insanity defense." *Id.* at 14.

[16] H.Tr.I at 153. Dr. Pepper also noted a 1973 diagnosis
that Wright "was suffering from a paranoid personality rather
than paranoid schizophrenia." *Id.* at 107.

[17] *Id.* at 146. Dr. Pepper also relied on the appellant's
ability to think abstractly, which evidenced lack of psychosis.
Id. at 108-09.

[18] *Id.* at 12.

[19] *Id.* at 19-20.

[20] *Id.* at 74 (Dr. Sack) ; *id.* at 157 (Dr. Pepper).

some kind of psychological disorder.[21] All three also
acknowledged the difficulty in distinguishing passionate
religious beliefs from mental illness.[22]

---

[21] Dr. Miller concluded that although the evidence permitted
alternative assessments, Wright suffered from psychosis, with
paranoid elements. H.Tr.II at 26-29. Drs. Pepper and Sack
both found Wright to suffer from psychological disorders that,
in their opinions, simply did not rise to the level of seriousness
required by the legal standard of insanity. Dr. Pepper concluded:

> I am not saying that Mr. Beachey Wright is okay. I am
> not saying that he is perfectly normal. I am not saying
> he functions as well as you or I. I am saying that he
> suffers from a personality disorder, paranoid personality.
> I am saying that he suffers from that, to an appreciable
> degree . . . . I have been invited to come to court today
> to state my views on whether this provided the substan-
> tial degree of impairment contemplated under the legal
> standard and my conclusion for all of the reasons I have
> stated was it did not.

H.Tr.I at 135-36. Similarly, Dr. Sack asserted:

> I don't deny this man was driven by forces within him,
> forces that represented in a turmoil, but I do not main-
> tain—I do not believe that he suffered from a psychosis,
> and on that basis, I concluded that he was responsible
> for his behavior, could form his behavior to the man-
> dates of the law.

H.Tr.I at 65-66.

Thus, the experts exhibited a range of views reflecting
their notions of the legal standard, see n.52 infra, and their
personal judgment. See also Davidson, Psychiatrists in Ad-
ministration of Criminal Justice, 45 J. CRIM. L., CRIMINOLOGY,
& POLICE SCIENCE 12, 14-16 (1954) (discussing diagnosis of
paranoid schizophrenia and paranoid personality).

[22] Dr. Miller remarked: "I think this is a very interesting
case, because it brings into bold relief some of the problems
that we have about deciding whether a person is either men-

The appellant, Beachey Wright, testified that he had been educated in a private Seventh Day Adventists' grammar school.[23] He described religious experiences starting while he was stationed with the army in Vietnam. After an honorable discharge, he attended college but left in 1971 because "God had told me to go and prophesy" about

---

tally ill or whether he is a 'religious fanatic.' I think, in Mr. Wright's case, that you can describe him as either." H.Tr.II at 43.

Dr. Sack was prompted to say, "I do not believe my psychiatric training and experience qualifies me to make judgment in that realm of thinking as to which religious beliefs are crazy and which are not." H.Tr.I at 16-17. He also compared the appellant's views with those of certain religious sects. *Id.* at 62, 69.

Acknowledging an element of religious compulsion, Dr. Pepper stated that Wright's ability to distinguish God's commands from human law indicated his ability to choose which to obey. He reported this statement made to him by appellant: " 'I will admit again that, if this thing is just in my imagination, then I am a sick man, but I don't believe that because of the firm faith in God, the kind of person that he is.' " *Id.* at 154.

Without explaining their reasoning or conclusions, the experts also debated whether appellant's claim to hearing God's voice stemmed from auditory hallucinations or inner convictions. *Compare* H.Tr.I at 54 (Dr. Sack) (inner convictions) *and* H.Tr.I at 92 (Dr. Pepper) (same) *with* H.Tr.II at 26-27 (Dr. Miller) (possible hallucinations; but critical factor is delusion). The appellant explained that the voice he heard

> is not physical but yet I hear it, not within my physical ear but yet it is a voice that speaks and it is clear and it is audible, but not in my physical ear. It is a voice that comes from within and I have attempted on numerous occasions to try and explain it and I am often misunderstood.

H.Tr.II at 62-63.

[23] H.Tr.II at 51.

God's plan to destroy the government.[24] He traveled to Washington, D.C. where he burned American flags in public places.[25] He returned to college, and then traveled again to Washington to perform his prophetic mission. His activities at that time led to an indictment, and ultimately commitment to St. Elizabeths hospital.[26] Wright said that after visiting religious colleges in the South, he arrived in California, where he worked as a construction worker. Then he left for Washington once more to fulfill his mission—and performed the acts giving rise to the instant indictment.

Wright told the court that he declined to raise the insanity defense not for fear of stigma: "I have a stigma of being an ex-mental patient, as it is." [27] Instead, Wright said he rejected the defense because

> the whole idea of the notion that I am suffering from some kind of mental illness is absurd to me. I know I express a great amount of religious conviction, more so than the ordinary person, but that is not in itself, as far as I am concerned, an indication of mental illness. I cannot accept a mental insanity

---

[24] *Id.* at 62.

[25] *Id.* at 63, 66-68, 70.

[26] *See* United States v. Wright, 511 F.2d 1311 (D.C.Cir. 1975). Wright's flag desecration conviction was overturned by the district court judge who found insufficient evidence of specific intent. *Id.* at 1312 n.1. After raising the insanity defense on its own motion, the court also rejected the conviction for destruction of government property, finding Wright not guilty by reason of insanity. *Id.* at 1312. The court of appeals then ordered Wright released from St. Elizabeths unless the government initiated civil commitment proceedings under the D.C. Code. *Id.* Wright was not subsequently civilly committed. Gov't Br. at 22-23 n.23.

[27] Wright was hospitalized at St. Elizabeths during 1974 following earlier charges. *See* n.26 *supra*; H.Tr.II at 83.

plea because it would be a compromise of my faith and the principles that have motivated me up to this point. It would discredit everything that I represent in coming here.[28]

D. *The Court's Order and the Trial*

The district court declined to raise the insanity defense over appellant's objection.[29] In its order, the court carefully reviewed the history of the case, acknowledged the conflict among the experts, and cited three related grounds for declining to interpose the defense. First, Wright was able to make "a rational and intelligent choice with respect to raising the insanity issue as a defense."[30] In support, the court noted the appellant's reliance "on a religious ground," on his own conviction that he was not mentally ill, and on his awareness of the possible consequences of raising the defense that could include commitment to St. Elizabeths.[31] Second, the court cited its own observations of defendant in court on at least seven occasions. Finally, the court found the testimony of Drs. Sack and Pepper "credible and believable" although in conflict with the views of Dr. Miller.[32] The court concluded that "Mr. Wright's decision to abandon and reject an insanity defense is not a product of any mental illness or abnormal mental condition but rather a considered determination on his part."[33]

---

[28] H.Tr.II at 76.

[29] Order, United States v. Beachey Wright, Criminal No. 78-309 (Nov. 24, 1978) *reprinted as* Appendix A to Appellant's Brief [hereinafter cited as District Court Order].

[30] *Id.* at 3.

[31] *Id.* at 3-4.

[32] *Id.* at 4.

[33] *Id.* Although the district court did not expressly cite the amicus memorandum, it similarly recommended that the court

At trial, the arresting officers and a detective gave evidence about the incident alleged in the indictment. One reported that the defendant spontaneously said at the time of arrest, "Jehovah had sent me." [34] The government also obtained testimony from an architectural historian about the value of the model and the cost of repairing both it and the glass display case.[35] Appellant, the sole defense witness, told of his mission to warn of God's pending judgment, and his use of symbolic acts as religious prophesy. The jury found appellant guilty.

At sentencing, the appellant asked for probation, promising that his conduct would not be repeated. He said, "I am not the usual criminal. I just—I am a man of great convictions and I have got to find other ways and means of expressing my beliefs and ideas about this." [36] The judge rejected his request and set the sentence. This appeal followed.[37]

II.

While knowingly violating the law,[38] the appellant apparently believed sincerely that he was selected to proph-

---

decline to inject the defense. Amicus Memo #2 at 6-10. Amicus counsel relied on 1) the objectively rational arguments against the defense in light of appellant's interests; 2) appellant's apparent ability to make a rational decision on the plea; and 3) the aims of sentencing.

[34] T.Tr. at 39 (testimony of Officer Travis Smith).

[35] T.Tr. at 76-77 (testimony of Anne-Imelda Radus) (model prepared at cost of $21,000; repaired at cost of $200; display case glass replacement cost of $117).

[36] Sentencing Proceedings Transcript (S.Tr.), Nov. 10, 1979 at 2.

[37] See n.1 supra.

[38] Wright testified that he knew he could be arrested for breaking the model of the capitol and he knew such an arrest could ensue because he broke human law. H.Tr.II at 82. He explained that "[i]n spite of the fact I realized what circumstances would ensue, I still recognize that I was acting under a greater power." Id.

esy God's disapproval of the national government.[39] Put this starkly, this case appears destined for a textbook discussion of the moral and political implications of the insanity defense.[40] For here the need to recognize religious or political expression competes with the criminal law's refusal to punish those who cannot fairly be blamed.[41]

---

[39] *E.g., id.* at 63, 66. Wright had this exchange with the prosecuting attorney:

> Q: Do you recall—at the time you broke the glass that holds the Capitol at the Capitol, that to do that would violate a civil law? You knew that was wrong, under the law, didn't you?

> A: Wrong? I was at that time acting as an agent of a higher power.

Id. at 81.

It remains unclear whether appellant believed he was free to disregard the prophetic mission. At times, he testified he had no choice. *See id.* at 66. ("I came back to Washington, D.C., because I was commanded to come back and reengage myself in the activities") *and id.* at 73 ("He urged . . . that He would not accept any excuses as far as my commitment to Him were concerned"). At other points, he indicated a decision based on his own conscience. *See id.* at 80 ("I believe in Him. I know that He has the power and the wisdom to direct my life . . . and I cannot, in good conscience, compromise that, that Faith.").

[40] This case bears a remarkable resemblance to a hypothetical example reprinted in a case book on law and psychiatry. *See* Livermore and Meehl, *The Virtues of M'Naghten,* 51 MINN. L. REV. 789, 841 (1967), *reprinted in* A. BROOKS, LAW, PSYCHIATRY AND THE MENTAL SYSTEM 115, 120 (1974) ("this patient has the delusion that he is a special agent of God and experiences auditory hallucinations in the form of divine commands"). That example was designed to demonstrate the difference between knowledge of moral and legal wrong for the purposes of the insanity defense.

[41] *See* United States v. Robertson, 507 F.2d 1148, 1161 (D.C. Cir. 1974) (Separate Statement of Bazelon, C.J.) (discussing "the ethical conflict between the individuals right to recog-

But no matter what we may think of these moral and political issues, the doctrinal treatment of Wright's claim is now fixed in our jurisprudence. Before this court is solely the narrow question of whether the trial court abused its discretion in refusing to interpose the defense over appellant's objection.

Counsel for appellant argues that "the testimony of Dr. Miller and Mr. Wright definitely raised a 'sufficient question' as to Mr. Wright's mental responsibility at the time of the alleged offense." [42] This claim is a reference to *Whalem v. United States,* where this court held en banc that

> . . . when there is sufficient question as to a defendant's mental responsibility at the time of the crime, that issue must become part of the case. . . . So, our query is whether in this case there was a combination of factors which required the trial judge to inject the insanity issue for, if such factors existed, his failure to do so is an abuse of discretion and constitutes error.[43]

At the same time, the court noted that "[n]o rigid standard exists to control the District Court in deciding whether it should require the insanity issue to be submitted. As a matter within the sound discretion of the District Court, this question must be resolved on a case by case basis." [44] To date, we have never overturned a District Court determination on this issue.[45] Nor have

---

nition of his protest and society's right to deny such recognition").

[42] Appellant's Br. at 27.

[43] 346 F.2d 812, 818-19 (D.C. Cir.), *cert. denied,* 382 U.S. 862 (1965).

[44] *Id.* at 819 n.10.

[45] We have approved both refusals to raise the defense, *e.g.,* United States v. Simms, 463 F.2d 1273 (D.C. Cir. 1972) (per curiam) ; United States v. Bradley, 463 F.2d 808 (D.C. Cir. 1972) (per curiam) ; Cross v. United States, 389 F.2d 957

we accepted guidelines proposed to limit district court discretion.[46] The reason for this continuing trust in the judgment of the district court is simple: the assessment of grounds for interposing the insanity defense is so fact-bound, so dependent on nuances of experts credibility and the defendant's presentation of himself, that the familiarity of the trial court is central to a sound decision.[47]

It is true that appellant's capacity to conform his conduct to the requirements of law at the time of the offense is doubtful. Compulsive aspects to his actions include his departure from a good job in California in order to perform a symbolic act in the nation's capital,[48] the repetitive nature of his prior similar acts,[49] and his spontaneous

---

(D.C. Cir. 1968) ; Trest v. United States, 350 F.2d 794 (D.C. Cir. 1965) (per curiam), and decisions to inject the defense, see United States v. Wright, 511 F.2d 1311 (D.C. Cir. 1975) ; United States v. Ashe, 478 F.2d 661 (D.C. Cir. 1973). We have, however, remanded for clarification or supplementation of the record where the trial court had not fulfilled its duty to explore the issue fully. See United States v. Snyder, 529 F.2d 875 (D.C. Cir. 1976) ; United States v. Robertson, 507 F.2d 1148 (D.C. Cir. 1974).

[46] See United States v. Robertson, 507 F.2d at 1158 (discussing Cross v. United States, supra, and Hansford v. United States, 365 F.2d 920 (D.C. Cir. 1966)).

[47] Appellant's counsel cites "criteria suggested" in previous decisions by this court. Appellant's Br. at 22. These include, for example, the "bizarre nature" of the crime and the probable success of an insanity defense. It should be clear that these and other factors were never intended to be determinative, but rather can be appropriately considered in support of particular analyses.

[48] See p. 5 supra. Dr. Miller included this fact as a basis for his conclusion that Wright suffered from delusions. H.Tr.II at 20.

[49] See n.26 supra. On cross-examination Dr. Sack was made aware for the first time of appellant's prior symbolic acts, which he conceded suggested a "driven repetive quality." H.Tr.I at 43. Dr. Sack reasoned that a driven quality could

statement to the arresting officer that "Jehovah had sent [him]." [50] The psychiatrist most familiar with appellant testified that appellant suffered from a mental disorder impairing his mental responsibility at the time of the offense.[51] The two other experts who disagreed with this conclusion in fact contributed testimony that would support the insanity defense.[52]

---

contribute to an expert finding of mental illness, but refused to modify his earlier statements that Wright acted from inner need, not compulsion. *Id.* at 44.

[50] T.Tr. at 39 (testimony of Officer Travis Smith). *See* p. 7 & n.21 *supra* (Dr. Miller's diagnosis).

[51] H.Tr.II at 9 (testimony of Dr. Miller). *See* n.10 *supra.*

[52] Both Drs. Sack and Pepper identified paranoid elements in Wright's thinking. *See* nn.16 & 21 *supra.* Providing yet another example of experts mistaking their proper role in court, both Drs. Sack and Pepper also indicated that their opinions were shaped by their understanding of the *legal* definition of insanity. Dr. Sack suggested that Wright's paranoia interfered with his judgment, and that some pathology was indicated in Wright's apparent desire to provoke confrontation with the law. H.Tr.I at 20. He concluded, however, "in the context of my previous experiences with the judicial system and answering the questions as posed by the Court Order, I would answer that question that he was not suffering from a mental illness that made it impossible for him to conform his behavior with the requirements of the law." *Id.* Similarly, Dr. Pepper found Wright suffers "to an appreciable degree" from a personality disorder, but concluded that this did not meet the legal standard for insanity. H.Tr.I at 135-36. This kind of testimony dims the hope of meaningful insights from non-lawyer experts. *See* Washington v. United States, 390 F.2d 444, 446 (D.C. Cir. 1962); Bazelon, *New Gods for Old: 'Efficient' Courts in a Democratic Society,* 46 N.Y.U. L. REV. 653, 659 (1971). Nonetheless, combined with the defendant's own testimony and demeanor, the experts provided sufficient descriptions of the defendant's mental and intellectual processes to permit the court to rule.

Nonetheless, there are also sound reasons for both appellant's and the trial court's decisions not to raise the defense. First, two experts testified that Wright did not suffer from a mental disease that substantially impaired his ability to obey the law.[53] Wright himself concurred,[54] and also indicated awareness that he knew at the time of the offense that he was breaking the law.[55] Second, there are sensible, logical reasons for assuming that this appellant would prefer a finite criminal sentence rather than an indeterminate commitment following an acquittal by reason of insanity.[56] The likely commitment would be to St. Elizabeths, an institution Wright knew for its poor— if not worse—conditions.[57]

---

[53] *See* n.21 *supra.*

[54] *See* pp. 10-11 & n.28 *supra.*

[55] *See* p. 11 & n.38 *supra.*

[56] Automatic civil commitment procedures are invoked in the District of Columbia when a defendant raises the insanity defense and is found not guilty on that basis. 24 D.C. Code § 301 (d) (1). That defendant then bears the burden of proving by a preponderance of the evidence that he should be released. 24 D.C. Code § 301 (d) (2). In an earlier case involving the instant appellant, this court held that these procedures *do not* apply where the insanity defense is raised by the court over defendant's objection. United States v. Wright, 511 F.2d 1311, 1313 (D.C. Cir. 1975). *See* n.26 *supra.* Civil commitment then can follow only upon the government's initiation and proof that commitment is necessary beyond a reasonable doubt. 21 D.C. Code §§ 541-544; *See* In re Bailay, 482 F.2d 648 (D.C. Cir. 1973). Dr. Pepper said that Wright understood that civil commitment, unlike a sentence following criminal conviction, could be indeterminate. H.Tr.I at 115.

[57] Wright was committed to St. Elizabeths before this court's decision in 1975. *See* United States v. Wright, 511 F.2d 1311 (D.C. Cir. 1975). Dr. Pepper reported that Wright did not wish to return to St. Elizabeths. H.Tr.I at 116. The quality of care at St. Elizabeths and the hospital's accreditation have had checkered histories. *See, e.g.,* HEW, Saint Elizabeths Hospital Initiative: Status Report (Sept. 1979).

Finally, Wright's expressed reason for rejecting the defense because it would compromise the principles motivating his actions is not irrational.[58] Two experts found his opposition to the defense not itself a product of mental illness.[59] The district judge had at least seven opportunities to observe Wright in the courtroom before deciding not to interpose the defense.[60] These considerations lend support to the district court's decision.

Most compelling, however, is the fact that the district court painstakingly followed all steps necessary to ensure full exploration of the insanity defense issue. The court ordered extra psychiatric evaluations in light of the initial St. Elizabeths report advising that Wright was competent to stand trial in spite of suffering from mental disease.[61] The court appointed amicus counsel, who effectively analyzed the procedural and substantive dictates of the law along with the evidence in this case.[62] At the two-day pre-trial hearing, the three experts and appellant each were examined at length by the prosecution, defense counsel, amicus counsel, and the judge. Finally, the judge fully expressed his reasons for declining to inject the defense,[63] including the credibility of the two experts and the appellant's opposition to the defense based on religious grounds and on his belief in his own sanity.[64]

---

[58] *See* pp. 10-11 *supra.*

[59] *See* p. 6 *supra.*

[60] District Court Order at 4.

[61] *See* p. 4 *supra.*

[62] The amicus counsel wrote two lengthy memoranda and examined witnesses at the pretrial hearing. This court suggested precisely this role for an amicus counsel when the trial court confronts a *Whalem* issue. United States v. Robertson, 507 F.2d 1148, 1158 (D.C. Cir. 1974).

[63] District Court Order at 4.

[64] *Id.*

As we interpreted *Whalem* in *United States v. Robert-son*, 507 F.2d 1148 (D.C.Cir. 1974), the trial judge is

> of course not bound to adopt in whole or in part the views of any expert. But no appellant court in our position can sensibly decide whether the trial judge has explored and exercised his discretion as required by *Whalem* unless the trial judge completes the exploration on the record and thereafter records in sufficient detail the reasons for his own expression of opinion.[65]

Because we find that the district court properly exercised its discretion in all respects, we affirm its judgment.

III.

The government has taken the occasion of this appeal to urge modification of *Whalem*,[66] which permits a trial court to impose the insanity defense over a defendant's objection. The government asserts that a defendant's

---

[65] 507 F.2d at 1161. We remanded in *Robertson* because the only testifying experts believed the defendant was mentally responsible, and they were not cross-examined. On remand, the district court heard testimony that led it to find sufficient evidence of mental illness affecting mental responsibility to consider the insanity defense. Further, the defendant had changed his mind and expressed a vigorous desire to raise the defense, permitting the court to avoid acting against the defendant's desires. Accordingly, this court directed the trial court to conduct a new trial. United States v. Robertson, 529 F.2d 879, 880 (D.C. Cir. 1976) (per curiam) (*Robertson II*). But during the voir dire of the new trial, the defendant changed his mind again. United States v. Robertson, 430 F.Supp. 444, 445 (D.D.C. 1977) (*Robertson III*). The district court received further expert testimony on the defendant's mental state and the court ultimately refused to impose the defense *sua sponte. Id.* at 447.

[66] The government argues that *Whalem* rests on "dubious authority" that cannot withstand recent developments. Gov't Br. at 16.

voluntary and intelligent waiver [67] of the insanity defense should *never* be overturned by the court.[68] Because we believe that *Whalem* better reflects the jurisprudential concerns underlying the defense, we cannot agree.

A. Alford *and* Faretta

The government urges this court to reshape the *Whalem* rule in light of *North Carolina v. Alford* [69] and *California v. Faretta.*[70] Neither case involved an insanity issue,[71] and for that reason alone their relevance is *de minimus.* When a criminal defendant's sanity is subject to question, doubt is cast not only on his competence to stand trial but also on the very capacity of our legal system to assign blame. The issue becomes whether there is sufficient question to require jury consideration of the defendant's ability to

---

[67] *Id.* at 17-25 (discussing North Carolina v. Alford, 400 U.S. 25 (1970), and Faretta v. California, 422 U.S. 806 (1975)). The government also points to a recent decision by the District of Columbia Court of Appeals, Frendak v. United States, Nos. 11042, 11046 (D.C.C.A. Oct. 24, 1979) (relying on *Alford* and *Faretta* to set "voluntary and intelligent" standard for accepting defendant's opposition to insanity defense). Even that court, however, reasoned that *Alford* and *Faretta* do not render *Whalem* unconstitutional. Moreover, we think the D.C. court's decision to depart from *Whalem* unpersuasive in the circumstances of this case. We treat its view in our discussion of the government's argument in this case.

[68] Gov't Br. at 65.

[69] 400 U.S. 25 (1970).

[70] 422 U.S. 806 (1975).

[71] *Alford* involved a defendant who wanted to plead guilty while maintaining his innocence, 400 U.S. at 37-38; *Faretta* involved a defendant who wanted to conduct his own defense, without appointed counsel, 422 U.S. at 834.

understand the law and conform his conduct to it [72]—that
is, whether he can be considered an autonomous, choice-
making actor deserving blame for alleged wrongdoing.[73]
Protection granted a competent individual's choice has no
bearing on this issue, which basically challenges the justification for punishment.

In this light, because *Alford* and *Faretta* protect rights
of competent defendants, their holdings have little application to *society's* obligation, through the insanity defense,
to withhold punishment of someone not blameworthy. A
plainly nonfrivolous challenge to a defendant's mental responsibility requires inquiry because it suggests that the
free will presupposed by our criminal justice system cannot be presumed. Thus, *Alford's* protection of a defendant's right to plead guilty, even while maintaining his
own innocence, cannot similarly reserve the insanity plea
decision to the defendant. Moreover, Alford itself is limited to permitting the self-claimed innocent's ability to

---

[72] As one scholar put it over two centuries ago, "[t]he
guilt of offending against any law whatsoever, necessarily
supposing a willful disobedience, can never justly be imputed
to those, who are either incapable of understanding it or of
conforming themselves to it." 1 W. HAWKINS, PLEAS OF THE
CROWN 1 (1716). *See also* H. PACKER, THE LIMITS OF THE
CRIMINAL SANCTION 133 (1968) ("to impose the moral con-
demnation of a criminal conviction on a person who is thought
to have acted in a state of severe volitional impairment
would be to abandon the notion of culpability in its most
crucial use").

[73] Acknowledging philosophic debates about the existence of
free will, Professor Packer has explained that the criminal
system operates *as if* human beings have free choice." H.
PACKER, *supra* n.72 at 132. He concluded, "[w]e must put up
with the bother of the insanity defense because to exclude it
is to deprive the criminal law of its chief paradigm of free
will." *Id.*

enter a guilty plea.[74] Certainly, this provides no authority for entrusting the entire decision on the insanity defense to the defendant.

Similarly, *Faretta's* explication of the "right to self-representation" [75] has no bearing on the insanity issue. No defendant, whether acting *pro se* or through counsel, can restrain the court from considering whether the insanity defense should be raised. Even the right to self-representation at trial does not grant license to reshape the very foundations of our criminal law.[76]

B. *The Role of the Defendant's Choice*

We cannot abdicate to the defendant the judicial duty to explore the issue once sufficient questions are raised.[77] Nonetheless, our reasoning does not disparage the importance of the defendant's preference to avoid the insanity defense. The inquiry by the court under *Whalem*

---

[74] Our holding does not mean that a trial judge must accept every constitutionally valid guilty plea merely because the defendant wishes to so plead. A criminal defendant does not have an absolute right under the Constitution to have his guilty plea accepted by the Court, . . . although the States may by statute or otherwise confer such a right.

400 U.S. at 38 n.11. The Court also directed that a self-claimed innocent defendant can submit a guilty plea only if he acts "voluntarily, knowingly and understandingly," *id*. at 37. Further, a factual basis for the guilty plea is necessary for the trial court to accept it. *Id*. at 38 n.10.

[75] 422 U.S. at 819, 834-35.

[76] The Supreme Court in *Faretta* expressly announced that the right to self-representation is not a "license not to comply with relevant rules of procedural and substantive law." 422 U.S. at 834-35 n.46. Thus, no defendant, acting *pro se* or through counsel, has license to avoid the criminal law's constant concern not to impose punishment where it cannot impose blame.

[77] *See* p. 13 *supra*.

necessarily includes exploration of the defendant's choice
and point of view. The line between mental responsibility
and irresponsibility may be thin, and errors falling on
both sides likely. The problem is especially treacherous
where the defendant justifies his conduct as political or
religious expression.[78] We know the danger of a Big
Brother state that treats its critics as mentally ill.[79]
When doubts about a defendant's mental condition remain
after a full inquiry, the strength and reasons for the defendant's opposition to the defense become all the more
important and may tip the balance.[80] This flexibility is
consistent with *Whalem*.

The government argues that the *Whalem* inquiry should
be replaced by a single question: Is the defendant's opposition to the defense voluntary and intelligent? [81] We believe this test, imported from *Alford*, would disserve the
necessary assessment of mental responsibility,[82] and would
in practice merely recreate the *Whalem* inquiry under

---

[78] *See* p. 12 & n.41 *supra*.

[79] For a powerful discussion of the political uses of psychiatric treatment in the Soviet Union, see H. FIRESIDE, SOVIET
PSYCHO-PRISONS (1979) ; A. PODRABNIK, PUNITIVE MEDICINE
(1979).

[80] The defendant's opposition to the defense may reflect his
understanding of his mental state at the time of the alleged
offense. It may also provide more general insight into the
quality of his reasoning. Finally, it may deserve ultimate
deference where insanity has not been established, and the
defendant's own dignity and decisionmaking require respect.

[81] Gov't Br. at 65. This is the standard adopted by the D.C.
Court of Appeals. *See* Frendak v. United States, Nos. 11042,
11046 (D.C.C.A. Oct. 24, 1979).

[82] *See* pp. 19-20 *supra*. It is also worth noting that *Alford*
and *Faretta* simply reaffirm longstanding principles. Their
holdings thus do not raise novel concerns unanticipated by
the *Whalem* court.

new and less candid labels. Under *Whalem*, the trial judge considers the defendant's opposition to the insanity defense and the quality of his reasoning.[83] The court may also weigh "the quality of the evidence supporting the defense," "the reasonableness of the defendant's decision to raise the defense," and "the Court's personal observations of the defendant." [84]

The government's proposed investigation into the voluntariness and intelligence of the defendant's decision by necessity bootlegs each of these considerations into the court's analysis. The proposed inquiry clearly extends beyond mere competence to stand trial. Such competence involves only minimal ability to understand the proceedings and assist defense counsel.[85] The proposed "voluntariness" criterion mandates assessment of the defendant's ability to decide how to plead, that is, his capacity to decide free from coercion from without or from within. In a real sense, a defendant lacking mental responsibility cannot "voluntarily" waive the insanity defense.[86] The

---

[83] *E.g.*, Cross v. United States, 389 F.2d 957, 960 (D.C. Cir. 1968) ("Although *Whalem* makes clear that the court must have the last word upon whether the insanity defense is to be raised, the defendant's wishes are highly relevant."). *See* United States v. Robertson, 430 F.Supp. 444, 446 (D.D.C. 1977).

[84] 430 F.Supp. at 446. *See* United States v. Simms, 463 F.2d 1273, 1277 (D.C. Cir. 1972).

[85] *E.g.*, Dusky v. United States, 362 U.S. 402 (1960). Experts tailor their opinions on a defendant's competency to stand trial to match these minimal abilities. *See, e.g.*, Letter from Dr. F. Jay Pepper to Roger Adelman, Assistant U.S. Attorney (Sept. 25, 1978), Government Exhibit #2 (Beachey Wright "is presently mentally competent to understand the proceedings against him and to confer with counsel to assist properly in the preparation and conduct of his defense").

[86] Often, mentally ill individuals do not or cannot acknowledge their illness. *See* O'Conner v. Donaldson, 422 U.S. 563, 584 (Burger, C.J., concurring).

"voluntariness" portion of the government's proposal thus inevitably turns to the strength of the possible insanity defense—and raises the matters covered in a *Whalem* inquiry.[87] The court must determine whether the defendant was free from delusion or psychosis in rejecting the defense.[88]

---

[87] There may be cases in which the defendant changes so markedly between the time of the alleged offense and trial that his condition at trial bears little relationship to his mental responsibility at the time of the offense. As a practical matter, and as demonstrated in this case, assessment of a defendant's mental condition when deciding how to plead is intimately connected to indications of his earlier condition.

[88] The requirement of a particularized competency finding is analogous to the trial court's duty to find specifically whether a defendant competently waived his right to counsel. Westbrook v. Arizona, 384 U.S. 150 (1966) (granting motion for leave to proceed in forma pauperis and petition for writ of certiorari). Similarly, our court has held that competence to stand trial alone does not establish competence to waive a jury trial, United States v. David, 511 F.2d 355 (D.C. Cir. 1975).

In the same vein, the Ninth Circuit has held more generally that a mere finding of competence to stand trial is inadequate to sustain the defendant's waiver of a constitutional right. Sieling v. Eyman, 478 F.2d 211, 214-15 (9th Cir. 1973). That court also approved language from an earlier dissenting opinion:

> Judge Hufstedler, in Schoeller v. Dunbar, 423 F.2d 1183, 1194 (9th Cir. 1970) has suggested the following standard: "A defendant is not competent to plead guilty if a mental illness has substantially impaired his ability to make a reasoned choice among the alternatives presented to him and to understand the nature of the consequences of his plea." We think this formulation is the appropriate one, for it requires a court to assess a defendant's competency with specific reference to the gravity of the decisions with which the defendant is faced.

Id. at 215 (footnotes omitted).

Similarly, the proposed "intelligence" criterion introduces *Whalem* concerns because "intelligence" must in-
volve more than evidence that a reasonable defendant
would decline the defense. The stigma and risk of confine-
ment associated with a successful insanity defense [89] provide grounds for always finding opposition to the defense
"intelligent." An "intelligent" decision in this context
must reflect the quality of the defendant's own reasoning
and the circumstances under which the plea decision is
made. Thus, the "intelligence" of the defendant's choice
can be determined only by an inquiry into the *merits* of
his choice—precisely the *Whalem* examination. Such an
inquiry considers the risks of both improperly assigning
criminal responsibility and unwisely imposing the insanity
defense against the individual's wishes.

Thus, in all likelihood, the approach recommended by
the government involves merely a minor—and perhaps
misleading—change in symbolic emphasis. By focusing
attention on the quality of the defendant's pleading decision, the government proposal tends to obscure society's
obligation to determine blame-worthiness before imposing
sanctions. Without hiding this obligation, a specific inquiry into the quality of a defendant's decision to waive
the insanity defense is permitted and encouraged under
Whalem. The trial court has authority to order a report
on a defendant's competency to stand trial [90] and on his
mental responsibility at the time of the alleged offense.[91]
So too may the court discharge its responsibility by pursuing specific expert evaluation of the quality of the defendant's decision to oppose the insanity defense. We have
not found *Whalen* and its progeny to stifle or distort the

---

[89] *See Developments in the Law—Civil Commitment of the Mentally Ill,* 87 HARV. L. REV. 1190, 1198-1200 (1974).

[90] 24 D.C. Code § 301 (a).

[91] Winn v. United States, 270 F.2d 326, 328 (D.C. Cir. 1959).

necessary inquiry; indeed, unlike the government's proposal, *Whalem* permits candid assessment of relevant factors.

C.   *The Decision Below*

Ultimately, the court itself must grapple with the dilemma posed by the limits of the criminal sanction and the risks of a paternalist state. As revealed in this case, the trial judge can ably confront this dilemma by drawing on experts and on the amicus counsel. The trial judge can give weight to the reasons proffered by the defendant, as he did here.[92] But such reasons cannot be determinative, anymore than can a bare finding of competency to stand trial. Instead, where a defendant opposes the insanity defense, but experts or the defendant's conduct before the court suggest the defense may be appropriate, the court must consider and explain its view of the defendant's competence to assess his own moral culpability,[93] and society's concern to punish only those worthy of blame.

Because we find such examination was competently completed and carefully explained below, we affirm.

So ordered.

---

[92] *See* pp. 10, 17 *supra.*

[93] The district court was ably assisted in this regard by the amicus counsel who urged careful exploration of "the quality of the defendant's decision not to raise the defense." Amicus Memo #1 at 13.

Appendix F:
Selected Bibliography

Allen, A.C. "Legal Norms and Practices Affecting the Mentally Deficient." *American Journal of Orthopsychiatry* 38 (July 1968):635-642.

Allen, R., and Rubin, J., eds. *Readings in Law and Psychiatry*. Baltimore: Johns Hopkins University Press, 1975.

Amarilo, J.D. "Insanity—Guilty But Mentally Ill—Diminished Capacity— An Aggregate Approach to Madness," *John Marshall Journal of Practice and Procedure* 12 (Winter 1979):351-381.

Anastasi, A. *Psychological Testing*. New York: MacMillan, 1967.

Arens, R. "The Durham Rule in Action." *Law and Society Review* 1 (June 1967):41-80.

_____ . *Insanity Defense*. New York: Philosophical Library, 1974.

Arens, R., and Laswell, H. *Make Mad the Guilty*. Springfield, Ill.: Charles C. Thomas, 1969.

Arboleda-Florez, J. "Insanity Defense in Canada." *Canadian Psychiatric Association Journal* 23 (1978):23-27.

Ausness, C.W. "Identification of Incompetent Defendants." *Kentucky Law Review* 66 (1977-1978):666-706.

Bazelon, D. "Psychiatrists and the Advisory Process." *Scientific American* 230 (June 1974):18-23.

_____ . "The Morality of the Criminal Law." *Southern California Law Review* 49 (March 1976):385-405.

Belli, M. "Insanity—A Lawyer's View." *Criminologist* 8 (Summer 1973): 20-28.

Bennett, D. "The Insanity Defense: A Perplexing Problem of Criminal Justice." *Louisiana Law Review* 16 (1956):484-496.

Blinder, M. "Understanding Psychiatric Testimony." *Judicature* 57 (February 1974):308-311.

Brakel, S. "Presumption, Bias, and Incompetency in the Criminal Process." *Wisconsin Law Review* 1974 (1975):1105-1130.

Caesar, B. "Insanity Defense—The New Loophole." *Crime and Delinquency* 25 (October 1979):436-449.

Ciruli, L.F. "Psychopath—The Law of the Boundary Line." *International Journal of Offender Therapy and Comparative Criminology* 22 (1978):80-90.

Cohen, H. "New Jersey Insanity Defense, Present and Proposed, Part." *Criminal Justice Quarterly* 1 (Fall 1973):214-223.

_____ . "New Jersey Insanity Defense, Present and Proposed, Part II." *Criminal Justice Quarterly* 2 (Winter 1974):38-53.

Colvin, M., and Sweeney, G. *Representing the Mentally Retarded—A Defense Lawyer's Manual*. Baltimore: Maryland State Bar Association, 1978.

"Competence to Plead Guilty." *Duke Law Journal* 7974 (1974):149-174.

"Criminal Law—Defense of Insanity." *Cornell Law Quarterly* 43 (Winter 1958):283-295.

"Criminal Law—Re-examination of Tests for Criminal Responsibility." *Michigan Law Review* 53 (May 1955): 963-972.

Curnow, D. "Legal Insanity and the Federal Courts—Does the Ninth Circuit Guide or Confuse?" *Federal Bar Journal* 33 (Fall 1974):305-321.

Danziger, C. "A Psychiatrist's View of Insanity as a Defense in Criminal Cases." *Marquette Law Review* 40 (Spring 1977):406-412.

Dershowitz, A. "The Law of Dangerousness." *Journal of Legal Education* 23 (1970):24-53.

Diamond, B. "The Fallacy of the Impartial Expert." *Archives of Criminal Psychodynamics* 3 (1959):21-46.

Diamond, B., and Louisell, D. "The Psychiatrist as an Expert Witness." *Michigan Law Review* 63 (June 1965):1335-1354.

Dix, G.E. "Death Penalty 'Dangerousness,' Psychiatric Testimony and Professional Ethics." *American Journal of Criminal Law* 5 (May 1977):151-214.

"Due Process and the Insanity Defense." *Notre Dame Lawyer* 53 (October 1977):123-140.

Fingarette, H. *Meaning of Criminal Insanity*. Berkeley: University of California Press, 1972.

_____ . "Disabilities of Mind and Criminal Responsibility." *Columbia Law Review* 76 (March 1976):236-266.

Fingarette, H., and Hasse, A. *Mental Disabilities and Criminal Responsibility*. Berkeley: University of California Press, 1979.

Flew, A. *Crime or Disease?* New York: Barnes and Noble, 1973.

Fowler, R. *The MMPI Notebook*. Notely, New Jersey: Roche Psychiatric Services Institute, 1972.

Gibbons, D. *Society, Crime and Criminal Careers*. Englewood Cliffs: Prentice Hall, 1977.

Gleick, J. "Getting Away with Murder." *New Times* 21 August 1978:21-27.

Goldstein, A. *The Insanity Defense*. New Haven: Yale University, 1976.

Goldstein, A.; Dershowitz, A.; and Schwartz, R. *Criminal Law: Theory and Process*. New York: The Free Press, 1974.

Goulett, H. *The Insanity Defense in Criminal Trials*. St. Paul: West, 1965.

"Guilty but Mentally Ill." *Journal of Urban Law* 53 (1976):471-496.

Guy, E.B.; Polsky, S.; and Heller, Mr. "Disposition of Mentally Ill Offenders." *Prison Journal* 48 (Spring/Summer 1969):24-33.

Hall, J. "Psychiatry and Criminal Responsibility." *Yale Law Journal* 65 (May 1956):761-785.

Halpern, A. "Use and Misuse of Psychiatry in Competency Examination of Criminal Defendants." *Psychiatric Annals* 5 (April 1975):96-122.

Halpern, A.L. *Insanity Defense.* New York: Insight Publishing, 1977.

Harriman, P. *Handbook of Psychological Terms.* Towata, New Jersey: Littlefield, Adams and Co., 1965.

Hays, J., and Ehrlich, S. "Ability of the Mentally Retarded to Plead Guilty." *Arizona State Law Journal* 1975 (1975):375-391.

Herman, J. "Constitutional Limitations on Allocating the Burden of Proof of Insanity to the Defendant in Murder Cases." *Boston University Law Review* 56 (May 1976):499-521.

"Incompetence to Stand Trial on Criminal Charges." *Mental Disability Law Reporter* 2 (March/April 1978):617-650.

"Insanity and Criminal Law in the District of Columbia." *Georgetown University Law Review* 44 (March 1956):489-506.

"Insanity Defense." *Mental Disability Law Reporter* 2 (March/April 1978): 651-664.

"Insanity and the Criminal Law." *University of Chicago Law Review*: 22 (Winter 1955):317-404.

Jeffery, C.R. *Criminal Responsibility and Mental Disease.* Springfield, Ill.: Charles C. Thomas, 1967.

Juren, N. "The Insanity Defense in Criminal Trials." *Suffolk University Law Review* 10 (Summer 1976):1037-1063.

Karpman, B. "On Reducing Tensions and Bridging the Gaps Between Psychiatry and the Law." *Journal of Criminal Law, Criminology and Police Science* (July/August 1958):164-174.

Keefe, J.F. *Eighth Annual Criminal Advocacy Institute.* New York: Practicing Law Institute, 1976.

Kerper, H. *Introduction to the Criminal Justice System.* St. Paul: West, 1979.

Kittrie, N. *The Right to Be Different.* Baltimore: Penguin Press, 1974.

"Law and Psychiatry—A Symposium." *American Criminal Law Review* 10 (Spring 1972).

Lindsay, P. "Fitness to Stand Trial in Canada." *Criminal Law Quarterly* 19 (June 1977):303-348.

Lowey, A. *Criminal Law.* St. Paul: West, 1975.

Lynch, G.P. "Insanity Defense." *Chicago Bar Record* 55 (March/April 1974):210-214, 216-217.

Matthews, A. *Mental Disability and the Criminal Law.* Chicago: American Bar Foundation, 1970.

MacDonald, J.M. *Psychiatry and the Criminal.* Springfield, Ill.: Charles C. Thomas, 1976.

McClay, W. "Impaired Consciousness—Some Gray Areas of Responsibility." *Journal of the Forensic Science Society* 17 (April/July 1977):113-120.

McConnell, J. "Doctors are People Too." *Michigan State Bar Journal* 47 (October 1968):12-25.

McGlynn, R.; Benson, D.; and Megas, J. "Sex and Race as Factors Affecting the Attribution of Insanity in a Murder Trial." *Journal of Psychology* 43 (May 1976): 93-99.

Menzies, R.J., ed. *Psychiatry and the Judicial Process*. Toronto: University of Toronto Press, 1979.

Morris, G.H. *Insanity Defense—A Blueprint for Legislative Reform*. Lexington, Mass.: D.C. Heath and Company, 1975.

Morrison, H. *Role, Function and Expectations of the Psychiatric Expert Witness*. New York: Practicing Law Institute, 1978.

Murray, H. *Thematic Apperception Test*. Cambridge: Harvard University Press, 1943.

Pasework, R.; Steadman, H.; and Pantle, M. "Characteristics and Disposition of Persons Found Not Guilty By Reason of Insanity in New York State, 1971-1976." *American Journal of Psychiatry* 136 (May 1979):655-660.

Peck, D.L. "Legal and Psychiatric Parody." *International Journal of Comparative and Applied Criminal Justice* (Fall 1977):173-179.

Pierce, C.M.; Mathis, J.; and Pishkin, V. "Basic Psychiatry in Twelve Hours." *Diseases of the Nervous System* 29 (October 1968): 533-535.

Poulos, J. *The Anatomy of Criminal Justice*. Mineola, N.Y.: Foundation Press, 1976.

Psychiatry and the Criminal Courts. Los Angeles: Los Angeles County District Attorney's Office, n.d.

Reisner, R. "Abolishing the Insanity Defense." *California Law Review* 62 (May 1974):753-788.

Ringer, L., and McCormack, J. "The Elusive Insanity Defense." *American Bar Association Journal* 63 (December 1977):1721-1724.

Roesch, R. "Competency to Stand Trial and Court Outcome." *Criminal Justice Review* 3 (Fall 1978):45-56.

_____ . "Legal and Judicial Interpretation of Competency to Stand Trial." *Criminology* 16 (November 1978):420-429.

_____ . "Determining Competency to Stand Trial." *Journal of Consulting and Clinical Psychology* 47 (1979):542-550.

Roche Psychiatric Service Institute. *The MMPI Booklet*. Newark, N.J.: Roche Psychiatric Service Institute, 1970.

Rubin, S. *Psychiatry and Criminal Law—Illusions, Fictions, and Myths*. Dobbs Ferry, N.Y.: Oceana Publication, 1965.

Samuels, A. "Mental Illness and Criminal Liability." *Medicine, Science and the Law* 15 (July 1975):198-204.

Schultz, J., and Thames, J., eds. *Criminal Justice System Review*. Buffalo, N.Y.: Hein and Co., 1974.

Silten, P.R., and Tullis, R. "Mental Competency in Criminal Proceedings." *Hastings Law Journal* 28 (March 1977):1053-1074.

Simon, R. *The Jury and the Defense of Insanity*. Boston: Little Brown, 1967.

Singer, A.C. "Insanity Acquittal in the Seventies." *Mental Disability Law Review* 2 (January/February 1978):406-417.

Sloverko, R. *Psychiatry and Law*. Boston: Little Brown, 1973.

_____ . "Developing Law on Competency to Stand Trial." *Journal of Psychiatry and Law* 5 (Summer 1977):165-200.

Sobeloff, S. "Insanity and the Criminal Law: From M'Naghten to Durham and Beyond." *American Bar Association Journal* 41 (September 1955):793-796.

Steadman, H. "Crimes of Violence and Incompetency Diversion." *Journal of Criminal Law and Criminology* 66 (March 1975):73-78.

_____ . *Insanity Defense in New York*. Albany: New York State Department of Mental Hygiene, 1978.

_____ . *Beating a Rap?—Defendants Found Incompetent to Stand Trial*. Chicago: University of Chicago Press, 1979.

Suarez, J. "Scope of Legal Psychiatry." *Journal of Forensic Sciences* 18 (January 1973):60-68.

Varga, J.M. "Due Process and the Insanity Defense—Examining Shifts in the Burden of Persuasion." *Notre Dame Lawyer* 53 (October 1977):123-140.

"Various Mental Disorders." *International Encyclopedia of the Social Sciences* 10 (1968):127-214.

Waddell, C.W. "Diminished Capacity and California's New Insanity Test." *Pacific Law Journal* 10 (July 1979):751-771.

Whatley, J. "Indigents and the Insanity Defense." *Law and Psychology Review* 3 (Fall 1977):115-134.

Wingo, H. "Squaring M'Naghten with Precedent—A Historical Note." *South Carolina Law Review* 26 (April 1974):81-88.

Yeager, N., and Consaluo, G. "Defense of Insanity—A Weapon of Oppression." *Catholic University Law Review* 5 (January 1955):182-189.

Yochelson, S., and Samenow, S. *The Criminal Personality, Vol. I*. New York: Jason Aronson, 1975.

Youh, H.E. *Clinical Psychologist—Neglected Witness in Insanity Defense Cases*. New York: Practicing Law Institute, 1978.

Ziskin, J. *Coping with Psychiatric and Psychological Testimony*. Beverly Hills: Law and Psychology Press, 1970.

Index

About the Authors

David M. Nissman is a deputy district attorney in the Lane County (Oregon) District Attorney's Office. Mr. Nissman is also a special lecturer at the University of Oregon law school. He received the B.A. from Emory University and the J.D. from the University of Oregon Law School.

Brian R. Barnes is a senior trial attorney in the Lane County (Oregon) District Attorney's Office. Mr. Barnes received the B.A. from Oregon State University and the J.D. from the University of Oregon Law School.

Geoffrey P. Alpert is the legal ombudsman for the Lane County District Attorney's Office and a special lecturer at the University of Oregon Law School. Dr. Alpert received the Ph.D. from Washington State University and has held faculty appointments at The University of Texas at Dallas and The University of Colorado at Colorado Springs. Dr. Alpert is the vice-president of the Western Society of Criminology and has published in numerous sociology and law journals.